The Amazing

Mail Order Business

and How to Succeed In It

The Amazing
Mail Order Business
and How to Succeed In It

by

Howard Sparks

Frederick Fell Publishers, Inc.   New York

New Printing, 1978

Copyright © MCMLXVI

by Howard Sparks

Library of Congress Catalog Card No. 66-17336

For information address:

Frederick Fell Publishers, Inc.
386 Park Avenue South
New York, New York 10016

Published simultaneously in Canada by:
Thomas Nelson & Sons, Limited
Don Mills, Ontario, Canada

ISBN 0-8119-0005-3

MANUFACTURED IN THE UNITED STATES OF AMERICA

2 3 4 5 6 7 8 9 0

To Vance R. Sparks,
brother and friend

CONTENTS

Introduction

The mail order business has been termed "America's last big-money frontier."

While the author of this book does not agree that mail order is the *last* opportunity through which an individual may achieve outstanding financial success, it does represent perhaps the only means by which anyone—regardless of location, social status, sex, race, or creed—may enjoy the chance to reap extraordinary rewards from a very modest beginning.

Unless you have had extensive experience in mail selling, there will be many questions in your mind about this fascinating way of doing business. It is the purpose of this book to answer the questions in your mind and to point out those aspects of mail order about which there can be no absolute answers.

This book is not meant to be a blueprint for organizing or developing a giant-sized mail order operation. Rather, it is intended to be a guide to the safe, sure establishment of a small business that will yield above-average returns through the sale of specialty goods and services.

The pages to follow will outline and explain the steps to take in the initial stage; will describe some of

the personal and financial requirements of a successful mail order operator; provide suggestions as to
what to sell; describe proven methods of making mail
sales; and point out those errors you should avoid.

In reading this book, bear in mind that mail order
work is a *method* of transacting business . . . and not
a *kind* of business. As in any other branch of merchandising, you are selling products to customers. The
only difference is that you do it with ads and printed
matter, instead of with counters and clerks. In all other
respects, the principles of good business practice that
apply to the latter will also apply to the former.

H. S.

The Amazing

Mail Order Business

and How to Succeed In It

Chapter 1

This Business Called Mail Order

You can get a dozen different definitions of mail order from a dozen different mail order people. But these definitions all boil down to a common understanding that 1) mail order is a form of merchandising not unlike the traditional retail-store type; and 2) this form of merchandising is characterized by the fact that all or a major portion of the orders for products are received by mail.

This definition may be a repetition of the obvious. But it is included here for the purpose of dispelling the aura of mystery and romance that usually surrounds the term "mail order business." Mail order is, beyond a doubt, the most exciting form of business activity. How else can you quickly generate a steady stream of letters, cards, orders, and inquiries from the four corners of the nation . . . and the world? But this intriguing facet of mail order is not enough to create or justify the myth that mail order is something set apart from the conventional channels of business.

Proof of this is that a large number of the most successful mail order operators were originally salesmen or those engaged in some form of sales work. Remember, mail order is *selling* . . . and the person who has knocked on doors and pounded the streets, or otherwise performed some kind of personal sales work, has a knowledge of sales techniques and principles that can be transferred to the mail order field. That so many salespeople have been successful in mail order confirms the adage that mail order is "salesmanship in print."

You don't, of course, have to have had personal sales experience to be successful in mail order work. Fortunately, there are many able mail-sales counselors and advertising agencies that can supply the proper sales approach to any given product or offer. The most important part of *your* job will be in selecting the right products (not an easy job, by any means); handling and filling the orders once they start coming in; planning additional offers to send out to your customer list; and—in the case of a rare runaway best-seller—banking the money.

The phrase "mail order" conjures up many different mental images in different people. Some automatically think of such gargantuan enterprises as Sears, Roebuck and Co. and Montgomery Ward. Others may visualize a spare room at home stacked high with shipping containers, incoming orders, inventory, etc., all devoted to the sale of one small item. Somewhere in between these two extremes there will be a manufacturer, wholesaler, or retailer who thinks of mail order in terms of an additional department for his business, to handle orders and inquiries that originate outside of his normal sales area.

Owing to its romantic appeal, mail order is a much-publicized business, and through magazine and newspaper articles the public has been led to believe that it is a quick, easy way to make a lot of money without very much work. What makes this belief tenable is that, as a matter of fact, a good many people have made a lot of money in mail order without very much work. (You may do so, too; but don't approach mail order with that expectation, for you may be sadly disappointed.)

The lot-of-money-with-very-little-work delusion has so captivated the popular mind that it has made many otherwise sensible people susceptible to sucker schemes and propositions. As a result, a host of clever racketeers have arisen to accommodate the gullible public by selling them worthless and exhorbitantly priced "plans" for going into the mail order business.

The obvious weakness in buying a ready-made mail order plan is that not only you but perhaps ten thousand other people bought the same plan, and the net effect is that everybody is trying to sell the same thing to everybody else. (This would not be out of place in China, where the ideal economy is one in which everybody subsists by taking in one another's washing.)

If you fall for one of these phony "plans" and open up a U.S.-style Chinese Washeteria, you'll probably develop a sour taste for mail order that no amount of chlorophyll gum will overcome. Therefore, when someone tries to sell you a stock mail order setup, remember that the chances of it working successfully are one in a million . . . and that chance is reserved for the racketeer who sells the plan to you and others like you. As we hope subsequently to prove in these pages, every successful mail order business is an *individual* proposition, one which the operater has designed and developed himself. And, with a little luck, perhaps we can show *you* how to carve one out for yourself . . . one that not every Tom, Dick, and Harry can muscle in on.

The attraction that draws most people to mail order is the intangible air of magic and get-rich-quickness that hearsay and publicity have created around it. Yet if you are a realistic person who demands more palpable reasons for entering a certain type of business, mail order offers plenty of those, too.

For instance, it is true that in mail order you are not faced with severe local competition. The nation literally is your market, and it's a big one—big enough to support thousands of prosperous mail enterprises, and big enough to accommodate many, many more. It is a vast market that hungers for an endless variety of products, whether they be unique, novel, instructive, entertaining, or merely utilitarian. The only thing *you* have to do to find your niche in this important phase of merchandising and distribution is to select a product or service which a large group of Americans need, want, and will buy. The rest is easy.

There are other good reasons for entering mail order besides the lack of competition. One of these is that your location has little or no effect on the success of your business. It makes little difference whether you live in Oshkosh or Fort Worth. (The first of these is the location of one of the nation's largest and most successful mail order gift houses. The second is the location of the largest mail order specialty firm of its kind in the world.) You might even live in an area as remote as Freeport, Maine, but don't let it bother you. Freeport, Maine—population 300—is the home of a world-famous sporting goods firm, whose sales run into millions of dollars per year, all made by mail.

Coupled with the advantages of a lack of competition and need for a special location, you also enjoy in mail order the freedom from having to meet your customers face to face. This does not mean, of course, that since you don't have to talk with them in person, you are at liberty to mistreat them. On the contrary, the need for courteous and careful handling of a customer is more pressing in mail order than it is in retail selling, because a mail order customer—particularly a new one—is frequently suspicious and wary to begin with. Only through prompt, scrupulous dealings with him can you convince him that your firm is worthy of his trust. Only in this way can you hope to build up an all-important "repeat" business.

What you realize from the above advantage is that you do not have to invest your capital in such things as store fixtures, cash registers, displays, clerks, and the many other overhead items that a store owner has to cope with. In mail order, you need no showcases except your ads and literature . . . no clerks but your sales letters . . . no cash registers but your deposit book . . . no inventory other than an adequate supply of the item or items you happen to be selling.

By now you probably agree that the advantages described are potent arguments for going into mail order, at least from your own point of view. But you may also be asking yourself, "What is it about people that makes mail order possible? Why do people go to all the trouble of ordering things by mail when it's so easy to hop down to the corner store and buy the same item?"

These are good questions and deserve good answers. In the first place, a lot of individuals *like* the idea of sending away somewhere to buy something. And even though this "something" may be as prosaic as a home haircut kit, there nevertheless is a thrill in anticipating its arrival and a thrill in opening the package. These emotional byproducts are usually absent when the purchase is made in a store.

Then, too, many individuals derive a feeling of personal importance when ordering by mail. Everyone likes and demands to be recognized as something more than a blank face in a sea of blank faces. Nobody likes to face the gruff clerk who gazes past you with steely eyes and says, "Whacha want?" as though your presence is a personal imposition. When a person makes out an order form, writes out a check, addresses an envelope, then he is getting a little of his own personality where it must get attention. When buying in person in most of today's modern stores, he is respected only for his cash and not for his identity.

There are other reasons that work to stimulate mail order buying. Such factors as age, transportation, and convenience foster mail order sales. Those who are old or infirm find it difficult to buy any other way. Those who are in a hurry appreciate the expediency of merely filling out an order form and dropping it in the nearest mailbox. Those who live in metropolitan areas may dislike the inconvenience of bus and subway travel to stores several miles away, especially when the item to be bought is of insignificant cost.

Another reason people buy by mail is that they simply don't know where else to get the item except from a mail order house. This reason touches on the only "big secret" there is in mail selling: exclusiveness. The best mail products are those that are not sold widely in stores. If yours is an exclusive product, one which you devise or make yourself, your customer cannot go anywhere else to get the item, because it is not sold by anyone but you. It is when you have exclusive control over the sale of an item that the nation truly becomes your market.

Some other motives for buying by mail are 1) that people like to be different from their neighbors, and ordering unusual products from distant places helps to achieve this feeling of difference; 2) that the customer believes he is making a cash saving over what a similar item would cost in a store; and 3) that he feels he is getting merchandise of better quality than he could obtain locally.

These are the important reasons why people buy by mail. You can probably think of some additional ones, but nearly all will fall within the framework of exclusiveness, ease-of-ordering, low price, and superior quality. As you examine various ideas and products for selling by mail, keep these reasons in mind and see how they apply to the idea or product selected.

Ultimately, the success of any mail operation hinges on one tremendously important fact—a fact which most of us take pretty much for granted—namely, that we in the United States have the best postal system in the world. It is this postal system which keeps us in business. The thought of a less efficient, less rapid handling of the mail and parcels is enough to give a mail order man a long siege of insomnia.

Contributing to our extremely efficient postal system, of course, is the fact that everyone speaks the same language. If you have ever traveled or done business in a foreign country, you know what an insurmountable barrier exists between people who cannot communicate with one another through the same language. That we have a common language in our country is not a business advantage you normally would give much thought to, but it is an advantage, and a very important one.

Our purpose in lauding the United States postal system in these pages is to bring to your attention the fact that the post office becomes your partner, your agent, and your counselor when you begin to sell by mail, and it is your privilege and duty to acquaint yourself with its many services. This won't usually be a chore. There are many things about the post office that you will find interesting, if not exciting, and there are many ways in which the personnel there can help you. In the succeeding pages you will find a resumé of the various postal services available and suggestions for taking advantage of them.

Every business is dependent on the postal system in some way, even though the business may not be a mail order firm. There are many types of businesses that sell entirely by mail, yet are not strictly considered to be mail order houses. Book publishers, for example, depend almost entirely on the mails to carry on their trade. Similarly, the writers who supply manuscripts to publishers are, in a sense, in the mail order business. Not only are books sold by mail, but magazine subscriptions are derived mainly from mail order promotions. It would be virtually impossible to attract and hold several million subscribers to a magazine if the job had to be done by personal salesmen. Because of their dependence on mail order selling, magazine publishers have done a great deal toward evolving successful mail-selling ideas which can be applied to other products.

Many specialized firms are in the mail order business because they cannot carry on their trade profitably by any other means. In this group are those who sell personalized services, such as the writers already mentioned, patent attorneys, and consultants of all kinds.

All of these—the publishers, the counselors, and those offering specialized services—when added to the conventional mail order houses combine to make mail order a vast business indeed. It is a business that can go in only one direction as long as the nation continues to grow and prosper, and that way is *up*. The more complex our society becomes, the more need for mail order firms to cater to new interests, new needs, new wants.

If you enter mail order seriously and studiously, with a willingness to learn, then your business has every chance to get bigger and better and more profitable. That's because the growth and expansion of our economy is an inherent force that works for—indeed, begins with—the individual businessman.

There are many people who are hard at work to get their share of the business, of course. Some of them do it one way, some another. And some do it by mail order. While you may not be particularly interested, especially if you are already experienced in sales work, it may be in order here to point out some of the other ways in which people are working to get the consumer's dollar.

The first and most predominant of these, as you know, is the retail store. Here the goods are displayed on shelves and in racks where they may be purchased on the spot. In addition, some retailers, especially those in the "hard goods" field, not only serve the walk-in trade, but also hire salesmen to work outside, visiting prospects in their homes and offices.

While this is going on, there are thousands of "specialty salesmen" out beating the brush constantly for sales and revenue. These are the door-to-door people, who sell everything from fire extinguishers to Bibles. Their products are sold neither through stores nor by mail order. They reach the consumer directly from the manufacturer, through the specialty salesman.

And while the retailers and specialty salesmen are at work separating the consumer from his money, the giant mail order houses such as Montgomery Ward are in there pitching, too. And they serve up a fast ball. Their catalogs are hard to resist; their sales terms are liberal enough to accommodate any pocketbook; and their variety of merchandise is perhaps the most extensive in the world.

In recent years, other merchandising innovations have crept up to divert the consumers' dollars in even more directions. One of these is telephone selling, where the sales spiel is given and the sale closed entirely over the telephone. There is more of this being done than you might think, especially in metropolitan areas. And it's probably more effective than you think.

Two other forms of selling are being exploited diligently by firms with the special know-how. These are radio and television. Techniques have been developed to allow complete sales presentations to be given profitably through these media, without any personal sales contact except the final delivery of the goods.

So there you have a brief picture of the merchandising scene as a whole. As you enter mail order, bear in mind that you will have to fight for your share of the business. You may not have any direct competition from other mail order firms, but you will have plenty of indirect competition from all those who have something to sell to the consumer in all the various ways just described.

You will have to do your fighting on several fronts at once. Not only do you have to have a good product, but you also have to have favorable selling prices, attractive terms in the case of high-priced items, and attractive sales stories that are imaginatively told. You have to deliver the exact goods that you advertise. You have to deliver them in a reasonable length of time. You have to guarantee them to satisfy—for if you can't guarantee them, you have no business selling them. You have to be able to accept complaints cheerfully and returned goods philosophically.

Above all, you have to keep an open mind. The

highway to mail order success is paved with the remains of people who, after one brief success, decided
they knew everything there was to know about mail
order. The most successful mail order men in the
country will be the first to echo the statement that
no one—but *no one*—ever completes his mail order
education. But by keeping your mind open, absorbing
each lesson as it presents itself, you can learn enough
to guide you through a financially rewarding mail
order career.

Chapter 2

The Personal Elements of Mail Order Success

You might think, with some justification, that mail order people are a peculiar race of humans who inhabit an exotic little world of their own, quite apart from the pathways of normal business and social life.

It is true that the nature of their business makes it possible for them to bypass conventional business intercourse and inclines them to look to other mail order people for social contact. It is also true that once they are plunged into mail order, it is indeed a world of its own, a world that few outsiders understand. It is a land where the mother tongue comprises a vocabulally of specialized terms, and any given conversation is likely to include a heavy sprinkling of such words and phrases as "pull," "pile up," "mortality rate," "cost per M," and "nixies."

But in spite of all this, mail order people are surprisingly like you and me, with no physical identifying marks that would set them apart, say, from a lawyer, an accountant, or a corporation executive. You can't tell a mail order man (or woman) by looking at him; you can only identify him by his work. And from his work, and how well he does it, you can draw a limited number of conclusions about successful mail order people. These conclusions are the personal elements of mail order success, and they partially—if not fully—explain why one person can pile up a fortune and another, with equal opportunity and facilities, sink swiftly into bankruptcy.

If you wish to measure yourself alongside these personal elements as you read them in the following paragraphs, that is your privilege. But don't assume because you may be lacking in one or more of them, that you are not suited to mail order. Rules are frequently broken, and in no other field are they broken with success as frequently as they are in mail order.

The first element in the personality of a mail order operator is the determination to have a successful business of his own, no matter how much work is involved or how many discouraging defeats he will encounter along the way. This may seem like a cliché to you, but without such firm, unwavering determination nothing of consequence can ever be built. It must exist first of all, even before a plan of action is laid out or other steps taken. A man with a great idea and no determination to see it executed gets exactly nowhere. A man with determination and no idea will eventually find an idea and the means to exploit it.

The second most important element in the make-up of a successful mail operator is the uncanny ability to smell out a potential money-making idea before someone else does. This ability is rare, but nearly everyone has a little of it in latent form, and it can be sharpened and refined through trial and error.

There is a set of standards by which to measure a promising mail order idea or product (given in a subsequent chapter), but this is only an aid at best. The most outstanding mail order operators seem to possess an intuitive sixth sense which tells them with remarkable accuracy which ideas will go over with the public, and which won't.

The ability to spot a winner before it has won is important in mail order work because there are literally thousands of products available to sell. The problem you will face is not in finding something to sell but in selecting from the myriad items already available to you.

You can see that this ability is far more necessary in mail order than it is in the case of a store owner who, on seeing a new item that strikes his fancy, merely orders a half-dozen, displays them on his shelf, and if his customers don't show any sales enthusiasm, simply marks the item down and takes a small loss. In mail work it isn't that safe. Once you select an item, you are going to take a much greater risk than a retail-store owner would to sell the same item. You will be investing in costly ad space, in expensive sales literature, and in postage. If the item doesn't capture sufficient interest and sales, you not only stand to lose the cost of the merchandise but your investment in ads, literature, and postage. This should be adequate proof that a nose for a "sure-fire" seller is a priceless thing to have, and that if you already have it, your success is not far off. If you have it in undeveloped form, it will come out as you go along.

The third personal factor in mail order success is the ability to plan. A mail order business requires constant planning, not only a master plan, but day-to-day plans, month-to-month plans. You have to plan your ads today in order to be sure they will be running the month after next. You have to plan now the kind of offer or product you will sell next summer, after winter sales have fallen off. You have to plan your mailings so as to systematically "work" your customer list. You have to plan the amount and kinds of printed matter you will need to service the inquiries and orders you receive from future ads and mailings. You have to plan shipping and handling facilities, capital and inventory needs, personnel requirements . . . and in mail order you nearly always have to plan these things well in advance. Arrangements have to be made, schedules have to be met, new schemes have to be set in motion. There is never an end to planning in mail order, and if you are not a planner—if you are a dreamer who is temperamentally opposed to planning today what you will be doing a month or a year from now—then it would behoove you to think twice about entering mail order. It is no field for the person who cannot or will not make plans and then carry them out.

Element number four is the ability to face the mail order business *realistically*, without kidding or deluding yourself. It is a business with certain romantic and intriguing aspects, but you can't function successfully in it by looking at it through the proverbial rose-colored glasses. You must hold all the facts up to the cold, hard light of truth. An extreme example of one who didn't is the beginner who ran across what appeared to be a sure-fire item which he could buy for twenty-five cents and sell for a dollar. "Why," he thought to himself, "can't I sell this product with post-cards? A thousand postcards ought to bring in at least a hundred orders, and at a dollar apiece, that would mean a $35 profit for each thousand cards I mail."

Well, it didn't turn out that way. Looking at it realistically, as an experienced mail order operator would do, we see certain fallacies in the beginner's thinking. In the first place, a thousand postcards will not pull a hundred orders for *anything*—no matter what it is. (It might pull that many inquiries or that many requests for a free premium, but not cash orders.) About the best such a mailing can do under the most ideal conditions is pull twenty-five to thirty orders per thousand pieces mailed. Also, our beginner failed to take into consideration the cost of printing the cards, getting them addressed, having the copy and illustration prepared, parcel post for mailing the orders to the customers, and other factors. All in all, had he gone ahead with this project, he would have lost money rather than making it, and a little hard-headed advance figuring would have shown him that this would be the case. (*Note:* Use of this example does not mean to imply that the familiar postcard is an effective or productive method for making a mail offering. Usually it isn't, as compared to other, more successful formats.)

Most successful mail order people will reveal a fifth element not too common among other types and classes of businessmen. This is the ability to use words effectively. Printing is the backbone of mail order; and the printed material, to do a profitable sales job, must have the right words thereon. Your career in mail order will be an endless stream of words—words for ads, sales letters, booklets, circulars, and many other kinds of literature. Some of this word-work can be obtained from commercial copywriters, but most of it will usually be done in your own office.

The more effectively you can use words, the more sales you can make. You don't, however, have to be a professional writer to get along with words. You don't necessarily have to have read a lot of books, and you don't have to bury yourself in the dictionary. But you do have to be able to state your thoughts clearly, without confusion or obscurity. This is particularly important in small-space magazine ads, where each additional word greatly increases the ad cost.

The best copy is that which is direct, concise, accurate, and sincere. Long, difficult words are "out" as far as mail order copy is concerned, because the typical mail buyer probably won't understand their meaning and will not go to the trouble of reading your ads or letters with a dictionary on his lap. The use of too many words is out, also. It isn't necessary or desirable to use ten words to say something that can be said in five. If you can make a complete sentence (and this isn't always a prerequisite), say what you mean, and say it with conviction and sincerity, then you will make out very well indeed in mail order work. If you are not sure you can do this, then make this experiment: Pick out several ads that particularly appeal to you, and with pen or typewriter copy these ads on a sheet of paper, word for word. Doing this at length will give you the feel of writing good ad copy. You can follow the same procedure in learning how to write sales letters.

There are other personal factors that contribute to the success of a mail order operator, but these can be, and frequently are, absent from a beginner who eventually makes good. One of these is the ability to save money and spend it wisely. Another is a personal history of successful endeavors, either working for someone else or working for yourself in some other field of business. Both of these elements, as we said, are frequently absent. Two of the nation's most profitable and successful mail enterprises are owned and managed by men who, in the beginning, neither knew how to save money, nor had had much personal success in their backgrounds. Until they brought their considerable imaginations and talents to mail order, both had, to a large extent, been personal failures. The magic of mail order enabled them to turn these deficiencies into assets.

For some time we have been discussing those things which are important to the personality of a successful mail order operator. Now perhaps you would like to know some of the things that are of no importance at all, although you may have been led to believe they were.

One of these nonimportant things is age. Within limits, age doesn't make a whit of difference in your chances for succeeding in mail order. That is possibly one reason why mail order is so attractive to men and women who have retired from active business life. It gives them an opportunity to remain active and earn some money at the same time, in a small mail enterprise. There are prominent mail order operators who will never see sixty again—several of whom didn't start their mail order careers until they were past retirement age. There are others working succssfully in mail order who are not yet thoroughly dry behind the ears. One of these, it seems, was running a nationally known firm by the time he was sixteen. (He had to close up shop to answer a draft call.) In between these extremes, you will find people of every age; in mail order it is never too early or too late to get started.

Sex is not important in mail work, either. Many firms, including the largest of its kind in the country, are being operated ably and profitably by women.

Education, in the formal sense, is one of the least important factors in mail order success. The special qualities needed in mail work are not the kind that are ordinarily taught in college. True, a grasp of certain specialized subjects can be very helpful (such as accounting and statistics), but the lack of it is no deterrent to a mail order career. It is what you learn *after* you get into the business that counts the most.

The last of the personal elements is experience. Most people who go into mail order go into it without experience in selling by mail, which is another way of saying that experience—although it could be an advantage to you—is not an indispensable requirement for mail order success. This is the one business field in which there is no such thing as experience which will qualify a person to slide effortlessly from one business operation into another, as is usually the case in other forms of business. In mail order the only kind of worthwhile experience you can depend on is the kind you get in building your own individual enterprise.

Chapter 3

A "One-Man" Mail Business and How Much You Can Expect to Make from It

If you regularly thumb through one or more magazines a month, you no doubt have been impressed by the rather bewildering array of mail order offers which shout their merits from every page.

Literally everything from soup to nuts is being successfully sold by mail. And in the event that you are not a habitual magazine thumber, it would be well worth the time and expense it takes to buy a few current issues of magazines and study them from cover to cover. You might start with *Popular Mechanics, Better Homes & Gardens, Progressive Farmer, True, Esquire,* and some of the Sunday papers that have national distribution. Your eyes will be opened to a range of mail order offers you wouldn't have believed existed.

In addition to the thousands of firms that sell their products and services directly through magazine ads, there are many more doing business by mail who don't use magazine or newspaper advertising at all. Instead, they sell by "direct mail"; that is, by letters and circulars sent directly to prospects without benefit of prior advertising or solicitation.

Should you already be familiar with the tremendous

scope of mail order, you may be slightly intimidated by it, and perhaps you are wondering whether, in a field that appears to be so crowded, there is room for *you*. The answer is an unequivocal "Yes." Instead of being discouraged by the great number of mail firms already active, you should take this as positive proof that mail order is a field in which many have found opportunity and profit . . . and there's always room for one more.

It may be a further source of encouragement to you to know that many of these firms, whose ads you see in magazine after magazine, year after year, are in reality small one- or two-man operations. Some of them are operated as spare-time enterprises by people who hold down regular jobs. Others are "seasonal" operations, whose owners work like the devil filling orders during the heavy mail order season (roughly from September through April) and spend the rest of the year doing very much as they please.

If you are really serious about mail order, you can make yourself a place in this exciting business. You will soon have unearthed a product or two which look good for mail selling; and with a little luck and a lot of courage, you'll be buying ads, shipping orders, and banking the money, too.

If you are primarily interested in the profit potential of the mail order business, one of the first questions you will ask is "How much money can I make?" This is a proper question; even though as a businessman you must have a genuine desire to serve the public faithfully and well, you must also have a burning desire to make as much money as you honestly can. That, as they say, is what it's all about.

Answering the question "How much money can I make?" is a lot like answering the question "How high is up?" It all depends on your own vantage point, your own definition of what "a lot of money" is. To some folks, $5,000 a year may sound like a princely income . . . enough to support an average family in modest style. To others, nothing less than $25,000 a year is worth troubling themselves about.

In the mail order field, you will find both extremes. There are one-man operations paying their owners $5,000 per year. There are part-time operations that supplement their operators' regular income, bringing in $500 to $2,000 a year. Then there are a group of companies that net their owners as much as $50,000 per year and more.

Unfortunately, however, it is only fair to point out that for every one of those mentioned above, there are many fledgling operations that earn little or nothing, for reasons ranging from too little capital to lack of essential business ability.

There is no pat answer as to how much money you can make in the mail order business, any more than there would be as to how much you could make in the dry goods business or the newspaper business. It depends primarily on *you* and what you do with the abilities, facilities, and resources you have.

If you are now holding down a regular job and are looking to mail order to supply an opportunity for part-time employment and income, you could not have

chosen a better field. For if you have a little capital
to invest and a few hours each day to apply to the
endeavor, you may eventually build a business that
will release you from your job completely. There are
few other forms of part-time activity that hold this
promise. Mail order is perhaps the only field in which
you can start a spare-time business on relatively little
money, without interfering with your steady job.
How do you get started in mail order? Again, there
is no precise answer. Everybody starts in a different
way. But everyone who enters mail order for the first
time usually follows a general pattern. First, you find
a product or service which you think people will buy
through the mail. Second, you decide where the largest
number of logical prospects for this product are and
which advertising medium (newspaper, magazine,
direct mail) is best for reaching them. Third, you
place an ad, or prepare a mailing, featuring your product or service. From that point on, the rest is pure
luck. You may make a young fortune from the first
ad, or you may not get enough orders to pay your
postage bill. But in either case, this is the way you
get started, and the outcome of this start is what
usually determines the balance of your career.

It may have occurred to you that you rarely ever
see a Help Wanted ad for experienced mail order
people. Similarly, you practically never see a going
mail order business advertised for sale. There are many
reasons for this. One of them is that every mail order
business is as individual as a toothbrush, and is not
adaptable to general use. Where one person can take
an idea and make it produce wonders, another person

might be a colossal flop trying to operate on the same idea.

Another reason you cannot buy a ready-made mail order business is that all those that are worth buying are so successful they are not for sale. (Except in the rare instance where the owner dies and there is no one to take his place.)

The best way to get started is to forget about buying a business which is already operating and concentrate on working up your own individual proposition. A good base from which to make this start is your own personality, interests, and tastes. For example, a man who was a former radio repairman is making a fine success of a mail order course in radio and TV servicing. A man who worked with sewing machines for years is doing extremely well selling courses of instruction by mail. A woman who was a working seamstress most of her life put her knowledge into a series of "how to" booklets and made a fortune. A fellow who preferred hunting to eating finally quit his regular job after thirty years and started mail ordering a little gadget which he had devised on one of his hunting trips. To date he has sold a million dollars worth of these gadgets by mail and has made more money than he ever could have in his job. A fellow who worked for years as a low-paid collection agent put his knowledge of collections into a series of printed collection aids and is now realizing $30,000 a year profit for his efforts—every penny made by mail.

You can easily see the moral in these illustrations. The best things to sell are the things you know best and like to handle best. The project you may now be pursuing as a hobby might hold the key to your mail order success. Or, perhaps the work you are doing for a livelihood is the thing that interests you the most, and there is some aspect of that work that can be developed into a product or service which could in turn be sold by mail to others of similar interest.

Perhaps you have no special training, but nevertheless enjoy handling certain classes of goods, such as fishing lures, office supplies, electronic gear. There certainly is a world of mail order opportunity in all those lines. Before you make a haphazard selection of something to sell by mail, first make a survey of yourself and then select those things that suit your interests and personality.

It is important that you make your initial selection of a product as carefully as you know how—especially if you are operating on limited capital and cannot withstand a serious loss at the start. You will be inclined, and perhaps urged by others, to jump right in with a hasty, ill-considered offer, on the theory that if this one doesn't sell, something else can be found that will. It is this frame of mind that is so receptive to the many worthless schemes and plans which are peddled promiscuously to newcomers by so-called counselors who want to help you "get into the mail order business" . . . for a fat fee. Remember as you search for a product with which to start that there are thousands of good products around to sell and hundreds of legitimate manufacturers and wholesalers who are ready and willing to supply them to you at good discounts.

Remember, also, that no sound business can be built on products which are not worth their selling price. Perhaps that is the main thing wrong with so many stock mail order setups: They require you to sell items for prices completely out of proportion to their real worth. As in any other business, you cannot be successful with an endless parade of one-time customers. To make money, you have to sell these same customers, time after time, either more of the same product or related products. And you cannot keep selling to them if they are not pleased with their first purchase.

Chapter 4

Mail Order Capital: How Much Is Needed and How to Conserve It

If we are to believe some of the ads in the mail order trade magazines, it is possible to set up a paying mail order business for an initial investment of $5, or $25, or some such small amount of money.

That's what they tell you, but don't you believe it. Nobody starts a successful mail order business with so little money. Few of these ventures have been started with as little as $100. Most of them were launched with sums ranging from $250 to $5,000, and the operators usually knew where to get more money in case they needed it.

There is no hard-and-fast rule about how much money you need to start a mail order business. It all depends on the type of product you will be handling, what selling methods you will use, and how elaborate your facilities are to be. A good general rule of thumb, however, is to have enough money on hand to finance at least a three-month operation, whether you intend to start in the most modest way or on a much larger scale. And if you have a rich uncle who can lend you enough money to finance the business for six months, so much the better. Under no circumstances should you start with only enough money to operate for the first three or four weeks. Not even the mail order business works well enough or fast enough to begin financing itself in so short a time.

Whatever else it is, mail order is also a gamble, despite the fact that you take every precaution to insure its success. Because putting money into mail order (or any other business venture, for that matter) is not unlike betting on the horses, you don't want to take any larger risk than is necessary. There are many ways you can reduce the amount of capital you need without instituting false economy measures.

You can, for instance, refrain from buying expensive office equipment and furnishings until you see whether your project is going over. Such things as filing cabinets, desks, and shelves can be improvised economically in the beginning from crates, boxes, and second-hand furniture.

You won't need a full-time secretary at the start; whatever correspondence is required can be done by part-time help or by your wife if you have one.

You will definitely need a good typewriter as you start your business, but you don't have to tie up precious capital in the purchase of a new one. You can either find a good used machine or rent one for a few dollars per month. Most office-supply firms will provide you with a typewriter on a rent-purchase agreement, under the terms of which you can apply your rental payments toward the purchase price of the machine if you decide you want to buy it later.

If you are on a regular job which pays you enough to take care of your living expenses and allows a surplus which you can divert into your business venture, you are in a fortunate position. In spite of the most careful planning, most new ventures require more capital than is anticipated, and you will be wise to begin thinking about where you can get additional amounts should you have a need for them.

The two largest slices of your available capital will usually be spent on 1) merchandise inventory; and 2) ads or direct-mail materials. You must have an adequate supply of stock to fill the expected orders from your first ad insertions or mailings. (This doesn't have to be a large inventory if you are in a position to get fast delivery from your supplier.) You don't want to keep your customers waiting for their orders; explaining why you haven't shipped the goods is more costly and time-consuming than shipping the goods.

The amount you'll need for ads or direct mail depends wholly on what you're selling and what type of magazine or mailing pieces will be used. In any case, it is good insurance to have enough money to carry you for the aforementioned three months. If you're using display ads, figure out what a month's advertising will cost; then set aside enough money to pay for it for three months. If you plan to sell by direct mail, figure out how many letters you can process and put into the mail per month and multiply by three.

There are two admonitions which perhaps should be injected here in regard to direct-mail selling. One is that printing prices are terrifically high, and to keep your cost-per-letter down as low as possible, it is necessary to buy your printed materials in fairly large quantities. By planning a three-month mailing in advance, you can place orders with your printer for the total three-month quantity and receive the most favorable prices. The second admonition is that your printing must be of good quality; this is one area in which you cannot afford to skimp or try to get by with anything less than the best. Shoddy, cheap-looking printing will hurt your sales substantially.

In selecting a product or products to sell by mail, it is usually a good idea at the start to choose those in the intermediate price range—those which retail for $3 to $10. To sell an item that retails for less than $3, you have to pull a great many orders in order to make a profit over and above your costs. It takes a lot fewer orders at $5 per order to break even or make a profit than it does at $1 or $2 per order. Which brings us to a mail order truth that is worth remembering: It is usually easier to increase the amount of money received per order than it is to increase the number of orders received, all other factors being equal.

As you may already have guessed, the price of a product has a great deal to do with whether it will perform profitably by mail, and this is true without regard to the merits of the product itself, particularly in the case of a big-ticket item. If you examine a cross-section of mail order products now being sold successfully, you will see that a preponderance of them fall within the $3 to $10 range. (This is not to say that relatively high-priced items cannot be sold by mail; as a matter of fact, many of them are, for prices ranging up to $100 and $200. But in the beginning it is better and safer to stick with comparatively low-priced units in the range given.)

In the event that you don't have enough money to get started in the kind of mail order business you want, it is wiser to postpone your plans until you have accumulated enough capital. You would be unusual if you were not impatient to get started, but it is a safer and saner course to go through a waiting period than to follow the riskier course of beginning on too little capital.

Many fabulous mail businesses have resulted from initial investments which now seem ridiculously low, but they have been the exceptions rather than the rule. On the other hand, many millions of dollars have been wasted in attempts to start mail order businesses by big-time investors who erroneously believed that mere quantities of money were all that was needed to create a profitable mail business.

Most established mail order firms have beginnings which lie somewhere between these two extremes. Over three-quarters of the successful mail businesses now operating, according to a survey, were started with more than $100 in capital. About a third of them were begun with at least $1,000. There is not much consolation in having to begin on such a modest scale as $100 or $200, but there is this to consider: The less money you have to start with, the better business-man you will have to be; the better you will have to plan; the more wisely you will have to spend. Succeeding in spite of a lack of capital will—in later years—

bring you as much satisfaction as you enjoy from scanning your latest profit statement.

The money you use to start a business-by-mail should not be borrowed money if you can avoid it. It should be money of your own to do with as you see fit, win or lose. Naturally, you don't want to deprive the wife and kiddies of the necessities of life while you're getting your stake together, for if you should then lose it in your venture, they'll never forgive you.

The time you spend while you're waiting for your savings to grow to a sufficient level should be time devoted to study. Learn all you can before you start. Read mail order books; watch the offers in magazines and newspapers; talk, if you can, with other mail order people. You will also find it profitable and enlightening to pick out a few ads from current publications; then check old issues of the same publications to see if identical ads were run in the earlier issues. (Most libraries contain back-number files of the more popular magazines.) If a product or service has been consistently advertised in a certain medium for a number of years, you can be certain that that product or service is a mail order winner.

If you propose to borrow money to finance your mail order venture, there are several loan sources you can consider. One is someone among your friends or relations who would consent to lend you the money without demanding an inordinate rate of interest and who would not be forever inflicting his advice on you. If you've got such a friend or relative, borrow as much as you think you need, and no more. Then work out a repayment arrangement that won't overburden your business during its crucial first few months.

The next best source for a loan is your bank. If you are an established, respected resident of your community, your chances of floating an adequate loan are good—especially if you have assets or property that can serve as security. On the other hand, if you are not well known to your bank, and have not had previous loan experience with your banker, your chances are pretty slight. Bankers as a whole do not understand the mail order business and do not lend money on mere ideas. Furthermore, banks hesitate to make speculative loans of any kind, except to big-time entrepreneurs who have already proved that they know how to use money to make money.

Don't assume from this, however, that you might as well give up the idea of trying to get the money from a bank. By all means, go ahead and try; you never can tell when a banker will be in the mood to say "Yes." Before you call on him, though, work up a type-written prospectus or outline describing exactly what you intend to do. This prospectus should clearly show what it is you plan to sell, how you plan to sell it, the amount of money you will need for starting inventory, the amount needed for ads or direct mail, and give a calculated guess as to the amount of profit you expect to realize from the effort. If you tell a convincing story and present a detailed, well-thought-out plan of action, you may get your loan on the spot.

Whether you need a loan in the beginning or not, it is not a bad idea to make a bank loan as soon as possible after your business begins to yield a profit.

The purpose of this is to lay the groundwork for larger loans you may wish to make in the future when you need to expand your operations. As you know, each succeeding time you borrow money from a bank and pay it back as agreed, you build a continually increasing line of bank credit that will be indispensable later on. For instance, one young man who started in the mail business went to his bank and borrowed $250 which he didn't need. He paid this back and shortly afterward borrowed $750. After about two years of additional borrowing and paying back money which he didn't need, this operator went to his bank and landed a $25,000 loan . . . which he did need. This, of course, was his objective all along, and it is through such foresight that small enterprises get to be big ones.

Chapter 5

How to Choose Products to Sell By Mail

Some years ago a mail order specialist gained a certain amount of fame by making the statement, "Anything that can be sold can be sold by mail."

To inexperienced persons this can be a dangerous generality. It is undoubtedly true that there are a few rare mail operators who are capable of selling virtually anything by mail—and doing it at a profit. But the average mail order man doesn't try it, nor does he need to.

To make it easy to enter mail selling without undue risk, there are a certain few categories of goods and services that come close to being ideal mail sellers; and, indeed, some of them could not be sold profitably any other way.

Before outlining these groups of sure-fire sellers, perhaps it would be in order to reiterate what was said a couple of chapters back about selecting a product. That is, the best thing for you to handle is something you like to handle. If you are a bookworm, you will probably be miserable attempting to sell sporting goods by mail. If you are an avid sportsman, you will rebel at the idea of selling books.

Generally speaking, you are most likely to be successful selling something which you create or make yourself, particularly if it has some originality or unique features about it. Similarly, your chances are enhanced when you sell something that is indigenous to your particular locale or region. For example, a Texas firm does a substantial business selling cactus plants by mail. In Texas, cactus is so abundant as to be a nuisance, but in northern areas of the country, where cactus isn't known in its natural form, people buy it readily. A Florida man does exceptionally well with sea shells, which are indigenous to his area. Nearly every part of the United States has some natural or manufactured product that is peculiar to it, and bringing such products to the mail-buying market at large can be very profitable.

If you are a talented person, you may be able to devise a mail order product or service based on your talent. For instance, if you are a musician, you can easily work up one or a series of instruction booklets on the playing of various musical instruments. These would be even more salable if you could think out and explain short cuts to learning to play. There is a great demand for information of this kind.

If you are a songwriter, you can turn out a course on how to write songs. There must be a million people trying to write song hits, and most of them are receptive to any information that will help them.

If you are a writer, you can put your knowledge of story, article, or poem writing into brief how-to manuals and sell them to aspiring writers through ads in the writers' magazines. There are any number of individuals doing this, some of whom are earning very respectable incomes.

If you are mechanically inclined, you can turn this aptitude into unusual gadgets for the home, shop, or car. Millions of consumers buy gadgets of all kinds, from magnetic cigarette holders to musical toilet-paper holders. If you could turn out an unusual gadget, you might be able to find a good market for it by mail. In this regard, don't attempt to make and sell a gadget that requires too much processing. Because if your orders suddenly multipled tenfold, you'd have a difficult time turning out enough of the articles quickly to fill the demand. Items that can be made by use of conventional power tools (drill press, shop lathe, etc.) are the best to begin with. It is not a good idea to start with a product that calls for the making of intricate dies, specialized jigs, and so forth. These things will eat up your capital before you know it.

In this discusion about products which you should handle by mail, it has been considered that you might already have a pet idea that you'd like to try by mail. If you have such a pet idea or project, by all means give it some serious thought, without paying too much attention to how silly it may sound to you. Some of the greatest mail order ideas have, in the beginning, seemed downright absurd, yet later turned into astounding successes. Don't let friends, relatives, or neighbors influence you. Their judgment in this matter is not likely to be worth much.

If you have an original idea, don't submit it to Mr. Schmaltz down at the corner drugstore for appraisal. Instead, locate a responsible mail order sales counselor and tell him about it. He'll give you a reliable picture of its possibilities and tell you how to go about getting it on the market. Mail order counselors (the good ones) will charge you a fair price for their advice; but, as you will discover, it is usually worth much more than what you pay for it.

If you don't already have something in mind to sell by mail, you'll have an interesting time unearthing a product. A good start is to determine the general class of goods which you want to handle (such as sporting goods), then subscribe to the trade journals which serve that field. These trade journals are real gold mines for the mail order operator, inasmuch as they contain announcements of new products as well as ads featuring all manner of items that can often be purchased directly from the manufacturer.

To illustrate the procedure for making a product-search, let's suppose you decide that you want to specialize in sporting goods. How do you find out who makes sporting goods and where to buy them? You could, of course, hop down to the nearest wholesale sporting goods house, if you live in a city, look over the many items available, and arrange to buy them at discounts. But if you don't live in a city, and you have no idea of how to get in contact with a wholesaler, the thing for you to do is to find out what trade journal serves the sporting goods field. (There *is* such a journal, and it is called *The Sporting Goods Dealer.*) In the pages of the trade journal, as we said, you will find every conceivable kind of sporting goods and gadget advertised by its manufacturer, distributor, or importer. Your job will be to select the item or items you want to offer by mail, get in touch with the manufacturer or other source, and arrange to become a mail order dealer.

The above method of uncovering a mail order product, or a series of products, applies to nearly all classes of goods in all fields of business. It is not the only method, but it is a simple, effective one. It requires a bit of patience, and sometimes a bit of sleuthing to get your hands on the right trade journals and manufacturers' catalogs—since in some cases these are strictly "inside dope" and are not to be meant to be read or seen by anyone outside of the field.

In selecting your line of products, keep in mind that there are certain rules to which the items must conform to be good mail sellers. In the first place— and this is very, very important—the thing you sell must have a long profit margin. By "long" we mean anything from fifty percent on up. (Sometimes even fifty percent is not enough.) Trying to sell on too low a profit margin can mean losses or failure of an otherwise good mail order offer. It is one of the common errors which you should avoid. You can see that a retail store can get along nicely with thirty-to-forty percent profit because it has a large variety of products and a relatively low selling cost per item.

But in mail order you have the additional expense of advertising and direct-mail materials. The cost of these has to come out of your gross profit. If your profit margin is too low, you won't have anything left for yourself after you've paid all the other costs. The fact that you have to have a long profit doesn't mean, of course, that your customer is paying more than he should for the product. There are many items available which you can buy for as little as one-third of their retail selling price, yet which nevertheless represent good buys for your customer.

Besides allowing you a good profit margin, the product you handle must have something out of the ordinary about it. It cannot be something that is sold in shops and stores to any considerable degree. If you look over a group of ads in any popular magazine that features mail order advertising, you will notice that in nearly every case the product advertised is one that is not available in stores. And it will have something unusual or unique about it to distinguish it from similar products.

If you have an analytical turn of mind, you may find it both interesting and instructive to study a hundred or so current ads in mail order publications and classify those hundred products or offers. Without actually performing this analysis, you can take our word for it that nearly every mail order proposition will fall into one of the following classifications:

1. *Information*—This comprises correspondence courses, books, manuals, monographs, pamphlets, etc. Most of these will have an instructional purpose: to show you how to do something, make something, or learn something. In the "information" phase of mail order, you'll find offers on a vast variety of subjects.

2. *Merchandise*—In this class will appear the gadgets, gizmos, gimmicks, and widgets of mail order. Things for the home, shop, car. The range of merchandise sold is very great, extending from fancy foods to drill presses to prefabricated houses to automatic lawn

sprinklers. A million and one different products make up the "merchandise" phase of mail order.

3. *Personal Services*—In this class will fall those specialized personal services by individuals who use the mails to promote their businesses, as described elsewhere in this book.

If you choose to sell merchandise, you don't have to have a startling new invention to be successful. Choose a product that is already being manufactured by someone else and start selling it. If it goes over, pick out something else in the same general class and offer it, too. If you sold a kit of small screwdrivers, for example, you could logically add other small tools which you'd sell to the same people who bought the screwdrivers.

Follow this pattern long enough, and you will eventually have a whole line of products which will then lend itself to being developed into your own catalog. In selling by mail, and especially in selling tangible merchandise which you buy from others, you won't make a tremendous amount of money selling just *one* item. To build a volume of business, and thus a sizable profit, you have to sell several different things—a *line* of goods. And once you've developed a large enough line, you can profitably switch from selling direct-from-ads or direct mail to catalog selling.

Perhaps the biggest single phase of mail order is the information selling field. The reason for this is not only that it is probably the safest and most profitable branch of the business, but also that it is the easiest to get into.

Information-selling requires little capital at the start

and in general yields a higher profit return than any other form of selling, for the amount of money invested. Most items in the information field are just so much printed paper, and the cost of the product itself may be as little as five percent of the selling price. It's the information that counts, and for which your customer pays—not the quantity of paper or number of words.

The market for various kinds of information is really vast, and helping to supply the demand is not only financially rewarding but a good way to render a valuable service as well. Thousands of people are thirsty for knowledge on hundreds of subjects. They want to know how-to-get-rich, how-to-win-friends, how-to-use-algebra, how-to-play-better-golf, and so on.

If you can give them the knowledge or information they want, you'll be well paid for the effort. You don't, of course, have to open a big correspondence school or go into the book publishing business. Your informational offering might be as simple as a twenty-five-cent sheet telling how to do card tricks, or a ten-page folio on how to make money doing any one of a hundred different things. The information you sell can be as simple or elaborate as you want to make it. There is a demand, and a waiting market, for all kinds.

The best way to break into the information-selling field is to write up your own material and have it mimeographed or printed in economical form. You don't have to have any pronounced literary ability. Just decide on a subject that you know pretty well, piece out your own knowledge by studying other books and courses on the subject, then write it up in clear, understandable language. Once written, the information is ready for publication. The method of reproduction is not too important as long as the finished product is attractive and easy to read.

The information field is perhaps the easiest one in which to build a line of related items. A person who buys one manual or booklet from you will buy additional ones on similar subjects if you have them to offer and if he was satisfied with his first purchase. With very little capital outlay, you can easily work up a series of small informational publications from which you stand a good chance of realizing an excellent income.

The number of subjects you can treat in this way is almost without limit. However, there are some general classes of information which sell better than others. The first of these is information on how to make money. Everybody wants to make money, and if you know of a way to do it, write your idea down and offer it through the mail. The most successful information sellers, as you can see by the ads, are selling information either directly or indirectly concerned with making money—in a thousand different ways.

Information on the various mechanical trades also sells well by mail. There now are—and always will be —plenty of people around who want to buy instruction manuals, books, and courses on how to repair automobiles, how to fix TV sets, how to build their own furniture, how to take better pictures, and similar subjects. If you have had sufficient personal experience in any one of the various trades, you might well work up a manual or booklet on the subject and offer it by mail. Don't let the fact that the same information is being offered by others stop you. In information selling there is always room for one more. This is particularly true of capsule courses of instruction, written to sell for a comparatively low price. For example, there are several high-priced courses on the market on the subject of radio and TV servicing. These courses sell for $150 and up. Not everyone is able to pay so much for a course in radio and TV servicing, so the way was clear for the development of a course to fill the lower-price gap. Along came a mail order firm with that very idea, and it is going over in a big way.

Money-making and the mechanical trades are the big leaders in the information-selling field. But there are many other subjects which sell well and offer opportunity to newcomers. The writing-instruction field, as previously mentioned, is always open for a new approach to the subject of writing-for-pay. Everybody at one time or another decides he is destined to write the "great American novel." The majority of these would-be writers never get beyond the doodling stage, but they continue to buy great quantities of booklets, books, manuals, courses, and what have you on how to write.

Other subjects that are grist for the mail order mill are how to learn shorthand, how to play musical instruments, how to learn touch-typing, how to become a public speaker, how to get into politics, how to get a Civil Service job, how to operate a collection agency, how to learn or do anything that will raise an individual's status and/or increase his income.

Akin to the information-selling field is the mail

order book business. The difference is that you sell books obtained from regular book publishers instead of writing and publishing your own. Conventional books sell by mail for the same reason that self-written manuals and courses sell. There are several advantages to selling books, not the least of which is that there are a vast number of titles to choose from, the product does not deteriorate, and you can usually set up a drop-ship arrangement whereby the publisher ships the books directly to your customer under your label. Another feature of handling books is the low postage rates which they enjoy. Ounce for ounce, a book travels cheaper than any other kind of product.

In selecting a line of books to offer, you will want to study the publishers' catalogs at length, selecting only those books that deal with money-making, self-help, and how-to-do-it topics. Most publishers will have several titles of this kind in their catalogs, and it is not too difficult to get yourself established as a mail order book dealer.

As stated previously, if you have a knack for making various objects in your workshop, you may find your mail order fortune there. This is especially true if you have designed or created a gadget which is distinctive for its originality or uniqueness.

Having such an original product provides you with exclusive control over the manufacture and distribution of it, and this exclusiveness is one of the great mail order success secrets.

If you don't have an idea, but nevertheless are handy with tools, give some thought to making and selling handicraft items of a more staple variety. Such things as gun racks, Lazy Susans, door nameplates, tie racks, lawn furniture, and toys often turn out to be good mail sellers. Sometimes you can even sell the patterns for making such items, for a good price, to people who have workshops and are looking for unusual things to make.

Aside from the handicraft line, there is one other big field of merchandise which lends itself to small-scale manufacturing and selling by mail. This is the chemical specialties field. What could be simpler than mixing up a few different chemicals according to a formula, packaging the final mixture under your own label, and selling it by mail? It isn't quite this easy; actually it is no trouble to produce various chemical products, but you may have some difficulty in selling them by mail. However, it has been done and continues to be done with great success every now and then.

If you want to go into chemical formulas, first study a few of the obviously successful mail order offers in the formula line. A cursory examination of a group of magazines and newspapers reveals several formula products that appear to be meeting with mail success. Some of them are fish-bait oils, arthritis remedies (be careful with this one), athlete's foot remedies, acne remedies, and cheap perfumes. There is nothing to getting into the chemical formula business after you've made a few contacts. You first decide on one of the products in the group which appeals to you most (perfumes, medications, etc.), then you get in touch with one of the advertising chemists whose ads appear in *Popular Mechanics* magazine and elsewhere (there are also some good books available containing hundreds of stock formulas), and pay him to supply you with the formula and preparation directions. Then you arrange to buy the raw ingredients in bulk, and bring in a supply of bottles, labels, and cartons. After you have made up a batch and gotten it neatly bottled and packaged, you start your ad campaign. If you were as lucky as one firm recently, you might run a $300 investment into a three-million-dollar business, practically overnight. But don't expect to duplicate this success. It doesn't happen often. You can, however, build a steady volume of business if you choose the right formula and put forth the right kind of mail order sales effort.

Chapter 6

How to Establish Sources of Supply

Finding one or more products to sell by mail can be as tough or as easy as you want to make it. If you close your mind, isolate yourself from the currents of trade information, and stand oblivious to the multitude of opportunities that constantly present themselves, you may well become a member of the chorus of mail order beginners who chant woefully, "But I can't find anything to sell by mail."

If, on the other hand, you are made of livelier stuff, you'll set your inquiring mind to solving the problem of something to sell, and will find more tempting opportunities than you will ever have time to try.

There are two general approaches to the problem of locating something to sell. One, you can determine the exact kind or type of product which you would like to handle, then go in search of someone to supply it. Or, two, you can go to a number of sources of supply without anything particular in mind, and from the variety of items thus examined, choose one or more of them to sell. One method is just about as effective as the other at the start.

Nearly everything manufactured in the United States for consumer use depends for its major outlets on the traditional retail store. (Although mail order is a "big" business, it represents only a very small part of the total volume of goods sold through retail stores.) To get the goods to stores efficiently and quickly, most manufacturers work through wholesalers. In general, the wholesaler buys the goods from the manufacturer for about forty percent of the final selling price. He in turn sells the goods to the retailer for about sixty percent of the final retail price. (In sales parlance, retail price is often called "list price," and the wholesale price is known as "net price.")

Now in the case of name-brand products, such as major appliances, certain brands of wrist watches, and so on, the wholesaler is often required by the manufacturer to limit the sale of these name-brand goods to specific "franchised" dealers. In such instances, the name-brand items are not usually available to mail order dealers, and it is largely a waste of time to try to handle such franchised products.

A wholesaler is within his rights to refuse to sell you certain classes of goods, because he owes it to his franchised dealers to protect them from as much competition as possible. Otherwise their dealership wouldn't be worth much.

Fortunately, though, most of the things that make good mail sellers are not franchised products but are items that a wholesaler will usually be glad to sell to any dealer who proves he is buying for resale and not for his own use. This includes mail order dealers.

Nowadays, there is more of a trend among manufacturers of specialty goods to sell their dealers direct, without going through the wholesaler. When this occurs, the manufacturer will in most cases sell to you at a somewhat higher discount than you normally would get from a wholesaler. There is no way of knowing which manufacturers will sell you direct, but it won't take you long to find out once you begin making inquiries.

Getting in touch with manufacturers is no problem if your town has a good library or Chamber of Commerce. Both these institutions customarily have copies of huge manufacturers' directories listing every important manufacturer in the United States, showing what he makes and where he is located. One of these directories is *Thomas' Register of American Manufacturers;* another is *McRae's Blue Book*. Both are extremely accurate and useful. Looking through these directories can be a revelation if you are not acquainted with the vast range and scope of manufacturing in the United States. And if you don't have any starting ideas for something to sell, a few hours spent thumbing through these books will give you plenty of ideas.

Should you find it inconvenient to have access to one of the directories mentioned above, the next best place to start on a product-search is in the telephone book. If you live in a small town, visit or write the nearest large city, asking for a copy of the phone book. In its yellow pages you will find listed all kinds of wholesalers and manufacturers offering all kinds of products.

In the yellow pages you'll find general merchandise

distributors who offer a thousand and one items under one roof, and you'll find specialized wholesalers who offer a related line of specialty goods.

Whether you visit your wholesaler in person or get in touch with him through the mail is not important. However, if you're completely new to the business, you might find it works out better to make your first contact by correspondence, then follow that up later with a personal call.

As far as possible, it is a good idea for you to establish sources of supply close to home, regardless of what you choose to sell. Once you get your business moving and the orders are coming in at a rapid clip, it is vital that you be able to get new supplies as quickly as you can in order to keep the orders going out.

Of course, there are many products (particularly imported ones) for which there will be no close-to-home source of supply. In cases of this kind, the only thing you can do is lay in enough stock at one time to meet your anticipated volume of orders for a considerable length of time. Then, as your stock dwindles, enter another order well in advance, in time to have the additional goods before you run out.

Up to this point, you have a pretty good idea of what a product search entails, and you have been given the most expedient methods for making it. (There are others, such as attending trade shows, following "new product" items in newspapers like the *Wall Street Journal* and *Journal of Commerce,* and studying import bulletins.) You have a good picture of how goods get distributed, and the confidence that somewhere in this distribution system there is someone who can supply you with what you want. From this point on, it is mainly a matter of writing letters, asking for catalogs, and thumbing through brochures until you finally locate the products that appeal to you.

There are several things you should know, however, about writing letters to manufacturers, wholesalers, and importers to establish sources of supply. One of these— a definite must—is to use an attractive, businesslike letterhead. To do otherwise types you as a rank amateur and unworthy of the supplier's attention. So before you start corresponding with any potential supplier, get a printer to work up a letterhead for you showing your business name, address, phone number, and other pertinent information. It doesn't have to be a fancy job, but it should be neat, well laid out, and be on a quality paper with envelopes to match.

Another requisite of supplier correspondence is the use of a typewriter in writing your letters. Even if you have to hire a public secretary to type your letters for you, it is well worth the small expense involved. A handwritten letter gets little or no attention in the hard-bitten, fast-moving business world of today.

In corresponding with sources of supply, make your letters as clear and straightforward as possible. If you want their catalog, ask for it. If you want net prices on certain items, designate the names and numbers of the items in your letter. If you are placing an order, state the quantity wanted, the name of the item, the catalog number, and the price you expect to pay. As a rule, a good supplier is a pretty busy fellow, and he will appreciate your keeping your letters as short and to the point as possible, without leaving out any pertinent information.

One final caution in regard to corresponding with suppliers: If you are starting a new business, or if you are an established businessman but are new to this particular supplier, you will usually get better service and faster delivery by offering to pay for your initial purchases in advance. Don't send an order in in the expectation that it will be delivered on "open account" unless you have been advised by the supplier that he will ship to you on that basis. Before he can do this, he will want to make an extensive credit check, and this takes time. Too, by paying cash in advance, you frequently can earn small extra cash discounts that add to your profit.

Chapter 7

How to Be a Good Buyer

In buying merchandise to sell by mail, remember that your efforts and attention should be directed toward buying those things *that will sell*, rather than to those things that you can buy cheaply. If you happen to find a product that offers both advantages, so much the better; but give your first consideration to salability, for if an item won't sell—doesn't have that all-important customer appeal—it wouldn't matter if you could get it for two cents a gross.

You have probably heard it said that there is more profit in being a good buyer than in being a good seller. To a large extent this is true, if by "buyer" we mean a person who can haggle and negotiate with a supplier until he has coaxed him out of another five percent discount. A retailer, for example, works on the assumption that there is a continuing market for his staple products. He knows, with almost absolute certainty, that eventually those ten bolts of broadcloth denim will disappear from his shelves into customers' hands. He doesn't have to force the sale of the broadcloth denim (through promotion) because the market is already established, and if he waits long enough, someone will come in and buy it. But in mail order you have no such assurance; your first concern is always, "Will it sell?" and secondly, "How much can I buy it for?"

There are, naturally, certain fundamental purchasing practices that you observe in mail order just as in any other line of merchandising. One of these is to buy in the quantity which will earn you the greatest discount, commensurate with your capital. If the regular discount on Product A is forty percent in dozen lots, and you can get fifty percent off in lots of six dozen, then you will want to order the six dozen—provided you have a reasonable certainty that they will be sold within a reasonable length of time. And provided further that in ordering the larger quantity, you do not have to dip into the funds that are earmarked for other purposes, such as advertising and postage. If you're on short capital, you're better off to pass up the extra discount and conserve your cash.

Another good buying practice is to take advantage of the extra discount you can usually get by paying cash for your purchases. This will range anywhere from one to five percent, depending on your supplier, but the usual cash discount is two percent. This is over and above your regular dealer discount.

At this point, it might be well to interject a caution in buying for resale by mail. That is, to steer clear of "closeouts" or job-lots of merchandise which you can buy at a fraction of their original cost. Goods of this type often make a quick profit, but it's a one-time profit, and when they're all sold, you are out of business, unable to get any further supplies at a comparable cost. (There are exceptions to this rule, as to all others, but it is a good one for the new mail order firm starting out with a small amount of capital.)

In the case of an item over which you have exclusive mail-selling rights (such as a product you make yourself), there usually arises the question of "How much will it sell for?"

The pricing of all goods is more or less arbitrary until they become so widely distributed that competition itself is the determining factor. In regard to standard consumer products, there is usually an attempt to relate the selling price to the actual cost of production and distribution, so as to yield a "reasonable profit." But in mail order, where you never know what your selling cost is going to be in advance, you meet with many occasions where you have to determine your own unit selling price.

In selling a standard product on which the retail price has been preset by the manufacturer, or has a more or less fixed value in the minds of the consumer, you would have to conform to this retail price should you offer the same product by mail. In such circumstances, all you can hope for is enough orders to cover your product, advertising, and incidental costs—and make you a small profit. Aside from aggressive promotion, there is very little you can do to put more profit into an item on which the selling price has already been established.

Where you are faced with the necessity of setting your own selling price on an exclusive product or offer, you will find a wider opportunity to build in some extra profit between the cost and selling price.

The "scientific" approach to arriving at a selling

price is to *assume* that you are going to move, say, one thousand units per month—which in itself is very arbitrary thinking, but is at least a starting point. Now if you expect to sell one thousand of the items—let's call them Widgetts—during one month, and they cost you fifty cents apiece (from the supplier, or to be produced in your own shop), then your cost of goods is $500. (Put that down on a sheet of paper.)

Next, you *guess* what it is going to cost you in advertising space and/or direct mail literature and postage to pull one thousand orders. Suppose your guess is $250 for the ads and letters. (Jot down $250.)

You then figure out how much it is going to cost you to pack and ship one thousand Widgetts. Include in this figure the cost of one thousand boxes or cartons, the cost of labels, wrapping paper, tape, stamps, and whatever else you will need. Suppose you figure it will cost ten cents each to put the Widgetts in the mail. That's another $100. (Write that down under the other figures.)

From there, you estimate all the other costs of doing business during this representative month. Such things as *your* labor for a month ($250) and the labor of a part-time helper ($100) should be considered. With this, you throw in the rent and utilities (another $50), and anything else you can think of in the way of overhead. Oh, yes. Don't forget $5 for the rented typewriter. Altogether, this chunk of overhead adds up to $405.

Now comes the pleasant part. You decide how much net profit you think you are entitled to (over and above your labor) during the month in which you filled one thousand orders for Widgetts and attended to all the other details of the business. How much did you say? $295? Well, that's fair enough. You earned it.

The next step is to add up all the numbers mentioned so far. If you wrote them down, it will be easy. If you didn't, here they are again: $500, $250, $100, $405, and $295. The grand total is $1,550.

Now all you have to do to find your selling price is to divide $1,550 by 1,000 Widgetts. And doing so reveals that each Widgett should sell for $1.55.

But now that we've arrived at a "scientific" selling price, somebody is sure to raise his hand and say, "Yeah, but how do we know for sure that $250 worth of ads will sell a thousand Widgetts?"

And someone else will ask the equally embarrassing question, "But isn't $1.55 an awfully unhandy, awkward price for a mail order product?"

And from the back of the classroom we hear someone else saying, "I don't give a hoot if we did figure it 'scientifically'; the Widgett looks like a good $2.00 worth . . . so why don't we sell it for that, instead of $1.55?"

To which any experienced mail order operator would answer, "Let's do!"

Chapter 8

To Build a Business, Build a Line

Unless you have a great deal of money to risk, and some prior mail order experience to go along with it, your first venture into mail work will center around a few carefully selected products. Most beginners start with just one item, and rarely more than two.

Restricting yourself to one or two offers at the outset provides a safe way of breaking into mail order while conserving your capital and giving yourself a chance to learn the business as you go along.

You will be tempted to try several different products or ideas at once, in the belief that such a "scatter-shot" approach is sure to bring in at least one winner.

But the newcomer is strongly advised to resist the temptation to begin handling several different offers simultaneously at the start—for two very good reasons. First, it is better to thoroughly promote one good item than it is to spread yourself too thin trying to promote several different items. One product well sold is worth half-a-dozen haphazardly sold. The second reason you should limit yourself at the start is that, as emphasized in an earlier chapter, it always takes more money than you think it does to start a mail order business; and even though you feel you have more capital than you need to push just one item by mail, it is better to let this item start showing a profit before diverting your extra funds into other offers.

You will, with some success at the start, soon pass through the one-item stage and ultimately reach the point where you have a *line* of products, which in the aggregate produces a much larger volume of business (and profit) than can ever be done with one product.

You may have heard stories about mail order firms that rack up sizable profits year after year from the sale of only one item. There are such firms. But they are in the minority, and a newcomer would do well to enter the field with the understanding that although he is advised against trying to handle more than one item in the beginning, it eventually will take a line of products to build a really worthwhile business. In the interim, he will be working and learning and testing, and by the time he is ready to start building a line, he will have the requisite mail order know-how to do it successfully.

You may be wondering at this point how you go about selling a whole line of products by mail. (To do it entirely with expensive ad space would require an enormous advertising budget.) There are a variety of ways of going about it, but the most usual one is to offer a "leader," which can be the first product you started with. This may or may not make very much profit in itself. To the people who buy your leader from small display ads or classified ads, you send circulars describing other products similar in nature to the leader. Experience shows that if your customer was satisfied with his initial purchase, he will continue to buy additional offers to a very profitable degree . . . so profitable, as a rule, that you frequently can afford to sell the leader even at a loss in order to accumulate the customer names to which you will send the additional offers.

One mail order operator runs his line of offers in a manner analogous to a string of circus elephants. Each elephant is led by the elephant ahead of him and, in turn, is leading the elephant behind him. In practice (and this works only where the products are very closely related in function or purpose), the use of each succeeding product depends on the buyer first having bought the offer ahead of it. Thus, the operator sells Item A, and shortly after he ships Item A, he sends literature describing Item B. As it happens, about eighty percent of the people who buy Item A also buy Item B. To the buyer of Item B, the operator sends literature describing Item C, and about fifty percent of the buyers of Items A and B also buy Item C. The process goes on indefinitely, until the operator has extracted every possible sale from his customers.

Other ways to merchandise a line of products are through a catalog, periodic mailings of bulletins and flyers, or by stuffing your envelopes with groups of small circulars, each describing a different offer. One nationally known firm does it with postcards. But instead of sending out one postcard, it mails one long postcard which is folded and taped around ten to fifteen smaller postcards to make a single mailing piece.

The catalog method is ultimately the most logical and most successful, but its main disadvantage is the high initial cost of preparation and printing. Nevertheless, it is the goal toward which nearly all mail order firms strive.

In building a line, there are several considerations you should take into account. One of these is that the additional items you add should be *similar in character* to your first or leading items, in order to make sure that your existing customers are good prospects for the additional items. Second, they should, so far as possible, be in the same general price range.

For example, if you succeed in selling a book on "How To Make Money" for $2, it is almost a sure bet that the person who buys it will be interested in buying a second book concerning money-making if it is priced in the same range. You wouldn't, obviously, turn around and try to sell the person who bought the money-making book a new kind of vitaminized bird seed or a revolutionary ignition system for hot rods. You would try to sell him more books related to the special interest he has already revealed by his first purchase.

Building a line, as in building any business, takes a great deal of time, thought, and work. It is a fairly simple process, but it can't be done hastily. Most of the beginners who fall by the wayside do so because they don't have the stamina and patience to sweat it out for the first tough year or two. Either that or they try to expedite their growth by shoveling money into too many projects at once, and find themselves under-capitalized, undermanned, overworked, and underpaid.

Businesses of all kinds are long-term propositions, and they should be accepted as such. Mail order is no different. Relatively speaking, mail order often pays off quicker than any other type of business, but rarely overnight, as you may have been led to believe. You can get rich in mail order, but you cannot "get rich quick."

The difference between reading of someone else getting rich in mail order and accomplishing it yourself is more a psychological one than a chronological one. When you read of a man who made a hundred thousand dollars in two years, your mind passes over those two years instantaneously, as though they were a mere snap of the fingers. But when you do it yourself, those two years can seem like a lifetime.

This is not to imply that you can make such a sum in two years, or any other specified period of time. But it has been done, and it will be done again. Too much depends on who you are, what you are, what your talents and experience comprise, how much money you have, and other factors to arbitrarily set a certain period of time in which you will progress from a humble beginning to a big-profit business.

Chapter 9

The Three Ways To Sell By Mail

In mail order there are three general techniques for
making the sale. All other methods are variations or
combinations of these three established methods. They
are 1) direct-from-ad; 2) inquiry follow-up; and 3)
direct mail.

Method One is the one with which you are probably most familiar. It is simplicity itself. You insert an
ad, either a display or classified, and use this ad to
pull orders directly. Such an ad will tell your sales
story in brief terms, quote the price, and ask for the
order. You can find innumerable examples of this type
of direct-from-ad selling just by glancing through any
one of dozens of popular magazines and nationally distributed newspapers.

Selling directly from the ad has several things to
recommend it, but it also has several disadvantages and
some severe limitations. The first of its advantages is
the one which lures most beginners to this method of
mail selling. That is, since the ad does all the selling,
you are not bothered with the expense and labor in
handling a lot of literature, circulars, envelopes, and
the like. Furthermore, this method is immediate. There

is no delay once the ad has been published. Each letter that comes in to you is sure to contain an order.

To employ the direct-from-ad method, about all you have to do is find a product, prepare an ad illustrating and describing it, then send the ad to the magazine or newspaper you have selected as the best medium. When the ad comes out, you will begin to get orders almost immediately, and they will continue for weeks, or possibly months—that is, if you're lucky. Sometimes an ad fails to produce a single order. Other times it will generate a young flood of orders.

The trouble with selling directly from the ad is that, for one thing, it's too expensive. Given a fairly good mail order product, you can usually develop more sales per dollar by employing the inquiry follow-up or direct-mail methods than you can by paying out large quantities of money for ad space.

For example, one firm has found that to sell its product—a gadget for hunters—directly from the ad requires $1 in advertising for each $2 worth of gadgets sold. In other words, $100 worth of display ads can be counted on to pull $200 worth of gross sales.

But on the other hand, this firm discovered after some testing that by running $20 ads (instead of $100 ones) which asked for inquiries only (instead of orders), and following up the inquiries with about $25 worth of printed literature, it did the same amount of business. In the first instance, it cost $100 to sell $200 worth of gadgets. In the second instance, the cost was only $45 to do the same selling job.

Our purpose here is to point out the merits and disadvantages of each of the three main methods of selling by mail—not to lay down any absolute rules about which is the "best," the "most profitable," and so forth. As we will attempt to convey here, and as you will learn as you get into the business, each product demands its own particular method. There are some products that sell best by direct mail, some that sell best by inquiry follow-up, some that can be sold most profitably directly from the ad.

In general, an item that is to be sold directly from the ad must be especially distinctive or unique in character, must be priced in the $3 to $10 range, and must be more or less an item over which you have exclusive control. In addition, it must carry a long profit margin (out of which you pay your ad costs), should be easy and inexpensive to ship, and should not be subject to appreciable breakage or deterioration.

An important point to remember when selling directly from ads is that the higher the price of the item, the more space you must use to get a profitable number of orders. An item that sells for $2, for instance, may produce a nice volume of orders from a one- or two-inch display ad space. But an item that sells for $5 would probably require three to four inches of space. And an item in the $10 range usually requires as much as a full column (ten inches) of display space. As the price goes up, so does the space necessary to sell the item.

Another consideration is that display ads (all ads for that matter) are seriously affected by seasons, much more so than the other two general sales methods. In general, a mail order display ad will start pulling profitably in the month of September, get progressively better toward November and December, and hit its peak in January. Then it will start slowing down gradually, and by May or June it will have pretty well exhausted itself. Not all ads behave this way, but a large percentage of them do.

In selling directly from the ad, you almost never get an adequate demonstration of the ad's pulling power on the first insertion. It's almost a sheer waste of money to plan on running such an ad for one time only. A good ad won't hit its maximum pulling rate until at least the third time it appears, except in very rare cases. So if you attempt to sell a product directly from the ad, by all means plan to give it a full opportunity to perform to its very best by placing it for three issues of the magazine or newspaper it is to be published in.

It is not unusual for an ad to pull several times as much business on its third or fourth insertion as it did on the first.

There are many classes of goods which lend themselves to direct-from-ad selling: gifts, self-help books, automobile accessories, sporting goods, and hundreds of others. Some notable direct-from-ad sellers have been slingshots, pepper mills, weather vanes, small radios, books on Judo and Karate, slide rules, fishing lures, recipe books, kits of all kinds, surplus parachutes, and plans for building low-cost homes.

Method Two, making sales by inquiry follow-up, is as widely used as making sales directly from the ad, and for just as extensive a variety of products. It is a simple method, and an extremely effective one if you have a worthy product and the right kind of sales literature to follow up with. Briefly, the *modus operandi* is to place a small ad, either classified or display (some firms use both simultaneously), giving just the main points of your offer in their most appealing form and asking the reader to send you a card or letter for complete information. On receipt of his request for more information, you send him the prepared literature, then wait for his order. If you don't receive his order from the first follow-up within a reasonable length of time, you can—as some firms do—send him another follow-up letter, this time with more urgency in it, and perhaps offering an extra incentive, such as a discount or a premium, for placing his order at once. Depending on the nature of your offer and the price tag it carries, you can keep following up an inquiry indefinitely until you have exhausted every possibility of making the sale. Some firms will send as many as ten different letters to an inquirer, but such firms usually are selling products which carry relatively high prices—in the $50 to $200 range.

The real essence of a good inquiry follow-up is powerful sales literature. It is no trick at all to get inquiries if your offer is the kind that appeals to a fairly large group of people. A small investment in small ads will bring inquiries in by the sackful. They're worthless, of course, unless your follow-up literature is strong enough to convert a profitable percentage of them to sales.

The principal feature of the follow-up method of selling by mail is to eliminate waste—waste in advertising and in sales literature. This waste normally is occasioned by the fact that in any given magazine audience there is usually only a small percentage of readers who are actual prospects for your offer. For example, a magazine may have a total circulation of four million copies, but out of that number of readers possibly fewer than a hundred thousand are actively interested in the thing that you are selling. To use a lot of display ad space to tell a complete story in such a magazine would be to address your message to 3,900,000 people who are not interested in your offer. This means that 97½ percent of your ad money has been wasted.

A far better way of reaching those among the readership who are prospects is to take the smallest size space that will accommodate the briefest possible message, and solicit inquiries only. By keeping such an inquiry ad going continuously, you will eventually reach virtually every prospect among the readership, at the lowest "per inquiry" cost.

The elements of a good follow-up are probably known to you already. If you have ever clipped out and mailed a coupon, or written a card or letter asking for more information about a product, you will recall that you got back an envelope containing these pieces: 1) a sales letter; 2) an illustrated circular; 3) an order form; and 4) a reply envelope. In addition, the letter may also have included a booklet, a premium coupon good for a discount or additional merchandise, a "testimonial" sheet, and possibly other items.

Now, if you want to operate a successful proposition by the inquiry follow-up method, your follow-up letter should contain all the above-numbered elements, plus whatever supplementary pieces you feel will help force the sale. These constitute the standard format for both inquiry follow-up and direct mail.

This is not the place to go into each of the various pieces in detail, but perhaps a brief description of each item's function would be in order at this point. The purpose of the first element, the sales letter, is to sell the prospect on the uses of the product concerned and dramatize the benefits it offers him. The letter tells him why he should buy the product, and buy it now—not later; it states the terms of purchase and the nature of the guarantee. It also clearly tells the prospect how to go about ordering the product: how much money he should send in advance and how to fill out the order form if it's unduly complicated.

The sales letter is not the place for, and rarely is used for, an actual physical description of the product itself. The letter deals only with uses, advantages, benefits, reasons why, terms, and guarantee. The description of the product is given on the circular. This is usually a printed piece, in one or more colors, illustrating the product, describing its physical features—dimensions, size, shape—and recapitulating the price, terms, and guarantee.

The other two elements, the order form and reply envelope, are self-explanatory. To get the most orders out of any given number of letters mailed, you must make it easy for your prospects to order. Bear in mind that not everyone keeps spare envelopes and stamps lying around the house, and a trip to town to pick up these things usually gives the prospect time to change his mind about ordering.

You must give your prospective customer an order

form, for if he is required to write his order out on his own stationery, he often forgets to include his street address, the quantity he wants, or something else pertinent to the order. Also, the inclusion of an order form in your follow-up serves to encourage the prospect to buy today, rather than put it off until a later time. Remember that many people are lazy and that the simple acts of having to write out an order and find an envelope to mail it in are enough of a chore to cause them to put off ordering indefinitely. The easier you make it for them, the more orders you'll get.

Nearly every good mail order product is adaptable to the inquiry follow-up method of selling, but some items lend themselves more readily to it than others. Products which are hard to describe in a few words, such as elaborate correspondence courses and technical goods, are best sold by this method. Products which are relatively high in price usually must be sold this way. On the other hand, items with a comparatively low price tag, i.e., $3 to $5, are most commonly sold by the direct-from-ad method.

The third general method of selling by mail is almost identical to the second, inquiry follow-up. The main difference is in the way names of prospects are acquired. In Method Three—direct mail—prospect names are gotten from sources other than publication advertising, and they are "cold" names, in the sense that these people have not taken the initiative in inquiring about your product or otherwise shown any active interest in it. The names you compile, rather than being "hot" interested prospects, are simply names of people whom you believe are logical prospects for what you are selling.

The sources from which you get these prospects' names and addresses are many and varied. There are mailing list houses who specialize in selling lists of names and addresses of persons who are likely to be prospects for nearly any class of goods or services. These list houses can give you thousands or hundreds of thousands of names of people who have bought books, gifts, courses, gadgets, and so on. Other sources for names are telephone directories, city directories, association rosters, and vocational directories, as well as other firms who are active in mail order and who are willing to sell you a list of their own customers. The latter practice is widely engaged in—where the list-users are noncompetitive—and can be extremely profitable for both parties. (A later chapter will deal with the development of a good prospect list in more detail.)

The direct-mail method of selling is exactly what its name implies. It is direct—from you to your prospect. No magazine ads in between. No cost of producing an inquiry. No time lost while waiting for an ad to come out. Selling by direct mail is simple in principle. You think you have a worthwhile product or service to offer. You think you know of a group of prospects who logically should be interested in buying it. So you sit down and write a letter to them and ask them to buy your product. That's direct mail—and anything else anybody says about it is just an elaboration of that simple formula.

Direct mail is one of the most astounding profit-making sales methods ever devised, provided you qualify it with a few ifs and buts. Few persons fully comprehend the power of direct mail to accumulate customers, and it may be just as well. The reason that more people don't fully understand it is that it literally has to be experienced to be understood. The source of that power is statistics and how to apply them to your mailings. You can operate successfully without a deep knowledge of statistics (or the "law of averages"), acquiring a working acquaintance as you go along, but any time you can devote to the subject of statistics and their application to the direct-mail business will be time well spent. (The Direct Mail Advertising Association publishes several papers or monographs on this subject which are well worth studying.)

Ideally, the direct-mail method would embrace a good product that is in demand by a large percentage of the population. The product would be one that measures up to all the standards of a successful mail order product, i.e., long profit margin, repeat potential, exclusivity, etc. *If* you had such a product, and *if* you had a direct mail solicitation that would pull a profitable number of orders, and *if* you could get a continuous supply of good names and addresses to which to send the offer, then you could get rich in short order—that is, if you could get enough postage money together to finance a mass mailing.

For example, suppose you had an item which ten million people logically would buy. Suppose further that you succeeded in developing a sales letter and circular that were good enough to bring you $50 profit every time you mailed a thousand letters. Given this ideal set of circumstances, you would have made $50,000 by the time you had reached only one-tenth of your total market. By the time you had mailed to the entire list of ten million people, you would have made a profit of $500,000! And by the time you had mailed the offer to every person on the list just one time, it would have been time to start mailing the entire list again. You would, in short, have what amounts to an infinite market, and with the law of averages guaranteeing your profit, the only thing between you and a fortune would be *time*. It does take a little time to process and mail ten million letters.

But, alas, such an ideal set of circumstances prevails about as frequently as Halley's comet comes blazing around the earth.

In practice, you can do very well indeed, if you are careful, even with a much smaller market, a reduced profit per thousand, and a much more modest mailing rate. It's being done all the time by firms who go along quietly year after year making money and creating steady customers by direct mail.

If you are brand new to mail order, you will do well to learn all you can about direct mail, but use it on a minor scale until you are sure you have enough capital to support a large, steady mailing campaign. For the beginner, direct mail is not as safe a bet as the direct-from-ad method or the inquiry follow-up method.

Chapter 10

Some Notable Examples
and the Methods They Use

The preceding chapter describes the three general methods of making sales by mail. With an understanding of these methods, the following examples can show you how they are put into practice by different firms selling different products. In reading over these examples, pay particular attention to whether the product is sold directly from the ad, by inquiry follow-up, or by direct mail; and see if you can determine why each particular method is used.

The first example is a big one: International Correspondence Schools. This world-famous company, as you know, sells thorough instructions in many trade and professional fields. The average cost of its courses to the student is probably as much as $250 to $300. The method of selling is inquiry follow-up only. Using display ads of many different sizes, in magazines ranging from *True Detective* to *Popular Mechanics,* the inquiries thus received are followed up by elaborate mailings, which spare no effort to describe and sell the course to the prospective student. In recent years there has been a trend among correspondence schools of this magnitude to follow up inquiries not only with mailings but with personal salesmen, but the inquiry follow-up in itself still remains the basic selling tool.

The Nelson-Hall Company, a book publisher in Chicago, sells a line of self-help books. These books are in the $2 to $5 range, for the most part. Each book is a complete course of instruction on such subjects as radio servicing, piano tuning, locksmithing, and self-improvement. Initial sales are made by the direct-from-ad method. Using full-page ads in mass publications such as *Science and Mechanics Magazine,* orders are pulled directly without benefit of follow-up. Each ad has a coupon with the different books listed by number. After a person has become a customer, he then receives, once or twice a year, a full catalog of the company's publications.

A man in Oregon has for years successfully sold a hair-growing remedy using the direct-from-ad method exclusively. Mediums used vary widely, from the *Saturday Evening Post* to the detective magazines. The ad is a full-page job, with order coupon, and hits directly for the cash order. Cost of the product to the buyer is $15. As far as is known, no direct mail or inquiry follow-up is used in making sales.

A company in Nebraska sells a pocket-sized radio. It is a self-contained set which sells for $4.99. It is sold directly from the ad. No inquiry follow-up or direct mail. Small display ads (about 2 inches in size) are used exclusively. The ad emphasizes the C.O.D. purchase, requesting that the buyer send only $1 initially, the balance to be paid on delivery. Magazines used are the mechanics and hobby group, fact detectives, and others reaching a male consumer audience.

A firm in Austin, Texas, prints and sells a line of colorful collection stickers, little gummed stickers bearing various collection messages, used by business firms to collect their past-due accounts. The average sale is about $7. No ads are used. Sales are made entirely by direct mail sent to business and professional people whose names are taken from the yellow pages of telephone directories.

A mail order firm in Newark, New Jersey, sells a line of gifts and specialty items in varying price ranges, but the average price is probably $3 per item. The firm uses both direct-from-ad and direct-mail methods. The direct mail takes the form of a catalog mailed to names of buyers rented from mailing-list houses. (It is also mailed, of course, to those people who order items direct from magazine ads.) Display ads do not ask for inquiries, but customers originating from display ads are followed up later with additional offers. The medium used is home-service magazines such as *Better Homes & Gardens* and *Family Circle*.

The L. L. Bean Company of Freeport, Maine sells a line of sporting goods, a few of which the company itself manufactures. The principal method of selling is to use a series of small display ads, each ad featuring a different product. These ads ask for the order directly, but also make the offer of a catalog. Products range in price from $5 up. Purchasers of items direct from the ad receive a catalog follow-up. Mediums used are the sporting and outdoor magazines, such as *Outdoor Life, Field & Stream,* and *Sports Afield.*

The Wham-O Mfg. Co. of California sells a hunting slingshot. The product sells for $1.50, and is sold directly from the ad. No inquiries are solicited. Ads are small display units in the sporting and outdoors field, as well as the mechanics and hobby group.

The Warner Electric Company of Chicago sells courses in electroplating, plastic laminating, and others. Courses are in the $30 price range. No attempt is made to get the order direct from the ad. Instead, large amounts of display space (with coupons) are used to pull inquiries, which are followed up by a complete direct mail presentation. This firm, in effect, sells complete plans for going into business for yourself and provides not only the instruction but the various tools and machines needed to put the plans into operation. (*Note*: Selling complete "turnkey" plans for going into business is a phase of mail order which has not, up to date, been overworked, and certainly offers a great deal of potential to the newcomer with a worthwhile idea for a small business plan that can be promoted by mail.)

An outfit in New York publishes and sells a directory of wholesale sources of supply. The directory sells for $3. The inquiry follow-up method is used exclusively. To get a volume of inquiries, both display and classified ads are used in such publications as *Popular Science, Science and Mechanics Magazine, Opportunity,* and *Specialty Salesman.*

An insurance company in Indiana sells life insurance exclusively by mail. Direct mail only is used. No personal salesmen. No inquiry follow-up. One letter tells the sales story, describes the policy, and gets the order. The policy is so devised that a twenty-five-cent remittance puts it into effect. The direct mailing contains an order blank and coin envelope for sending the initial twenty-five-cent premium. Names of prospects are bought from mailing-list houses.

The Dollar-A-Month Plan of Philadelphia sells a course of instruction and materials for conducting a local independent bookkeeping service for small businesses. The course and franchise sell for about $30 and are sold by direct mail only. The Plan uses lists of known opportunity-seekers, but does not use ads or inquiry follow-up.

A New York firm sells a book of business plans describing the essentials of 137 different small business ideas. The book sells for $4. The inquiry follow-up method is used, with inquiries pulled from classified ads in the mechanics and opportunity magazines.

The U. S. Stationery Company of New York sells a line of office equipment and supplies, such as steel cabinets, desks, ball-point pens, and card files. Uses direct mail only. No ads are used; no inquiry follow-up. Direct mail takes the form of a series of postcards, each card illustrating a different offer and containing a built-in order form. Lists are obtained from list houses and rented from other large direct-mail firms. At intervals, customers are sent a catalog.

The Haband Company of New Jersey sells neckties and slacks by mail. It uses direct mail only, which is sent to lists of known mail order buyers. No other method is used. Average sale is about $7.

There you have fifteen examples of well-established, nationally known mail order firms, what they sell, and the methods they use to sell it. These examples are given in brief form, but sufficient information is given to enable you to understand why a particular method is used for a particular product. The fact that all of these firms are reputed to be highly successful ones (some of them doing millions of dollars worth of business per year), and the fact that their success was won entirely by mail, proves that they wisely adapted the right mail selling method to their respective products.

Choosing the right method is another of the all-important "secrets" of mail selling. Many projects have failed through lack of careful selection of the method to use. Some dealers try to sell directly from the ad, when they should be using direct mail. Others use direct mail when they could sell more profitably direct from the ad. Others could be profitably using all three methods, yet are limping along on just one.

We have tried to indicate and emphasize that each individual product or offer demands its own method, and that there is no pat formula for determining which is the best method to use, short of trial and error. Discovering the best method for *you* to use is partly a process of reason, based on factors previously outlined, partly a matter of experience, but largely a matter of *testing*. Test one method; then test another. Now test them together. Then revise the copy and test them again. Test them for the best seasons, the best ad mediums, the best sales-letter copy. Test the price, the terms, and the guarantee.

Even after a series of tests has pointed the way to the best sales method to use for your product, you should continue testing to see if you can improve the results you are getting. Some things to try are larger ads, different headlines, longer sales letters, more colorful circulars, the use of premiums, the inclusion of testimonials from satisfied users, and all the other elements of the offer that lend themselves to variation, improvement, and change.

Testing is expensive, but not testing can be even more expensive. One advertiser was advised by his agency to change a few words in an ad to capitalize on a different appeal. "No soap," said the advertiser. "That would mean another ten dollars for a new engraving." About a year later the agency succeeded in making this minor change, and the pull of the ad increased twenty-five percent. Since this ad, running consistently in several magazines, pulled about $20,000 worth of business a year, that "minor" change in copy was worth exactly $5,000 to the client. Thus, in the preceding year, to save $10 in engraving costs, he had cheated himself out of $5,000 by refusing to test.

Chapter 11

Advertising Media: When and How to Use Them

If you have a product which you think will sell, but you don't want to attempt to sell it by direct mail or the inquiry follow-up method, there are three general ways in which to bring it to the attention of a great many prospective buyers.

These three ways, or media, are 1) magazines; 2) newspapers; and 3) radio and television.

Radio and TV as media to produce volume mail sales have been profitably exploited by several firms with the expert know-how required. Conversely, they have been tried by many firms that did not have the special knowledge or experience, and severe losses resulted. For the beginner's purposes we would rule them out altogether, unless the beginner has plenty of money to risk and plenty of mail selling experience to back it up—in which case he wouldn't be a beginner.

With radio and TV out of our way, we have only two media left to discuss. We'll consider these in the opposite order of their importance to the mail order aspirant. Newspapers as a mail order medium are, to a large degree, ineffective, expensive (reader for reader), and short lived. Any one of these reasons is enough to discourage the use of newspapers. However, there are a few exceptions. These are the big metropolitan papers that publish Sunday supplements, special out-of-town editions, and mail order sections. This group of papers is used consistently by many mail dealers with good results. Some of the papers so used are the *Chicago Tribune,* the *New York Times,* the *Los Angeles Examiner,* and the *Chicago American.* A complete listing of them here would serve no constructive purpose. If you live in handy proximity to a well-stocked newsstand, you can find any number of them there. In fact, it might pay you to buy a few of them and study the Sunday mail order sections. You'll get some idea as to what is being sold and what may be sold via newspaper advertising.

Using the mail order or "shopping" sections of the metropolitan papers has both advantages and disadvantages. One of the advantages is that an ad can be placed and published in a very short span of time. This is a considerable advantage when you are in a hurry to test a new ad or product. Whereas you frequently have to wait six weeks to three months for your ad to appear in a magazine, you can submit it to a newspaper one week and it will be in the readers' hands the next. Rarely does a newspaper require you to wait more than two weeks for your ad to appear.

A second advantage of using newspaper space for mail order is that it provides a good proving ground for new products and different ads at relatively low dollar outlay. Before splurging a large amount of money on ad space in a big national magazine, you can often test the offer with reliable accuracy in the shopping sections of the newspapers. Naturally, the results you would get from such a test would be more indicative than conclusive, but they would tend to show weaknesses in the offer or ad copy, which could be corrected before placing more costly ads in magazines.

The products that will sell well from newspaper space are usually the same ones that will sell from magazine space. However, a preponderance of products sold through newspapers are utilitarian—items which have a practical use—such as gadgets for the kitchen. Another group of these offers is in the health and patent medicine fields. There is one outstanding feature of any product that can be successfully sold through newspapers, and that is that it must definitely appeal to a mass audience, since newspaper audiences are not selective, screened, or specialized as is the usual case with a magazine readership.

The disadvantages of using newspaper space for mail selling are first-cousins of the advantages. The fact that an ad can be published in a newspaper without too much delay also means that newspapers are quickly prepared, and just as quickly read and thrown away. Even if you use one of the special weekly editions, the life of the ad is much less than it would be in a monthly magazine. While a newspaper ad will pull for two or three weeks, a magazine ad will often pull for three months or more. The reason for this is simply that newspapers are discarded soon after they are read, whereas a magazine will lie around the house or office for months, and it frequently is read and reread by several people other than its owner.

Another disadvantage of newspapers is that they

do not offer an opportunity to do selective selling, as previously pointed out. They are edited and published for indiscriminate masses of people. If you tried to reach a specialized group of prospects—dentists, for instance—through a newspaper ad, most of the circulation for which you paid would be wasted. The number of dentists among any newspaper readership is mighty small, perhaps less than one-tenth of one percent. It would not be good advertising practice to pay for ten thousand unwanted readers in order to reach ten you did want. A far better procedure is to spend your ad money in the pages of a dental trade journal, where every reader is a dentist.

It is this quality of selectiveness, combined with widespread circulation, that makes magazines the best all-around mail order medium. For magazines—as opposed to newspapers—are edited for specific groups of people who have certain interests and characteristics in common.

Because magazines are aimed at specific groups of people, however large they may be, the magazines themselves can be classed in definite groups by their editorial characteristics. As a future mail order operator, it will pay you to learn these groups of magazines in a general way, although nothing will be gained by your knowing the names of every magazine in every group.

Nearly all magazines suitable for mail order purposes can be classed in the following groups: general family magazines, farm magazines, vocational and hobby magazines, and trade journals. There are other groups, such as the "quality" magazines edited for intellectuals; "religious" magazines and papers edited for various religious organizations and denominations; and the scientific publications edited for scholars, scientists, and teachers. Inasmuch as these latter groups are not suitable for mail order advertising, there is little point in your giving them much study.

The general family magazines are edited and published for the family group in the middle-income bracket. If you could isolate and examine a typical subscriber to one of the family magazines, you'd find he was married, had a wife and a couple of kids, owned his own home, earned somewhere around $5,000 per year, and was for the most part a pretty average guy. You'd find that the general magazine to which he subscribes is so written and edited as to interest in some way every member of the family above diaper age. Some examples of the largest family magazines are *The Saturday Evening Post, Life,* and *Look.* Curiously enough, while the family magazines are great ad media for standard-brand products sold in stores, they usually perform very poorly for mail order offers, or their advertising rates are so high that they preclude use by the average mail operator. If you study a current copy of any of the magazines mentioned, you will find only a few, if any, mail order offers in their pages, for the reasons mentioned.

Closely akin to the general family magazines are the adult consumer publications edited on a male and female basis, each catering to the interests of the respective sexes. These magazines, on the contrary, are usually very good mail order media, and are used extensively to sell a wide variety of mail order goods and services.

In the mail group are such magazines as *True, Esquire, Saga,* and *Argosy.* In the female group are *Glamour, Living for Young Homemakers, Seventeen, Modern Bride,* and others with a slant toward the modern woman.

Then there are the so-called shelter magazines, which comprise an excellent group for mail selling purposes, particularly items in the gift-and-gadget line, products for the home, garden, or workshop. Among these are the familiar *Better Homes & Gardens, House Beautiful, House & Garden,* and *American Home.* A study of the ads in the mail order section of any or all of these publications would be worth the time expended, because many of the advertisers shown are very successful and their techniques worth emulating.

The farm magazines, as a whole, are also very good mail order advertising media. The reason for this is obvious. Rural people are isolated, to some extent, from city life, and their principal contact with the urban world is through farm papers and magazines. It is in the advertising columns of rural publications that they are able to keep track of new products and services and find new things of interest to them.

Many mail order firms depend almost wholly on farm publications for their sales. Naturally, to use these publications profitably, you must have a product or service which fills a rural need. Among the items being successfully sold to this market are film-developing services, plants and bulbs, formula compounds, tools, cutlery, Bibles, seeds, and building plans. There are many magazines in this group, varying widely in editorial content and form, but some of the better-known ones are *Progressive Farmer, Capper's Farmer, Grit, Farm Journal,* and *Farmer-Stockman.*

In the vocational and hobby group (including the science and mechanics magazines), we have perhaps the most productive mail order media available for an extensive variety of products and services. These magazines are edited for people who want to learn how to do various things, who want to extend their range of practical knowledge, with or without the profit motive.

In this group are the so-called mechanics magazines, which show their readers how to construct things, how to repair things, and how to understand scientific and mechanical things. Whether for amusement, amazement, or profit, their readers want to learn. It is this group that is the most receptive to mail order offers related to their interests, and you have only to look at a specimen magazine for proof of this. Every conceivable kind of book, tool, gadget, course of instruction, and plan is being offered. Some of the leading publications in this group are *Popular Mechanics, Popular Science, Mechanix Illustrated, Science & Mechanics, Workbench,* and *Crafts and Hobbies.*

Similar to, and partially overlapping those listed above, are the hobby magazines, both special and general. There are specialized hobby magazines edited specifically for such fields as photography, model trains, and stamp collecting; and there are those aimed at the hobby field in general. These, like the mechanics magazines, are excellent mail order media for products that cater to their readers' interest.

The final group with which we are concerned is the trade journals. This group comprises a vast array of publications serving every business and professional group. Each of them is written and edited along the lines of interest of each particular business, trade, or profession. There are trade journals for barbers, trade journals for motel operators, trade journals for bankers, dentists, doctors, lawyers, druggists, florists, garage mechanics, bill collectors, architects, and operators of service stations, and hundreds of others. These journals provide a tailor-made medium when you wish to sell a specialized product to a specific group of prospects. There are dozens of flourishing mail order concerns who operate no other way. To delineate all of them would take more space than we have here; it should be sufficient to say that as an aspiring mail order operator, it will be worth your time to learn more about the field of trade journals, as well as the other groups of mail order publications. The most expedient way to do this is to get hold of a recent copy of the Standard Rate & Data directory for "Business Publications." You should also have the SR&D directory for "Consumer Magazines," as well as their newspaper directory if you plan to use newspaper advertising. Copies of these famous directories may be purchased from the publisher, Standard Rate & Data Service, Inc., 5201 Old Orchard Road, Skokie, Illinois. Or, if an advertising agency will be handling your ads, it will have these directories on hand for your use.

Chapter 12

How to Use Magazine Advertising to Build a Mail Order Business

Many mail order firms depend almost wholly on magazine advertising to secure their orders and inquiries. Indeed, without magazines, a newcomer would be out of luck, because the use of them represents almost the only way a new firm can get started safely and on little capital. In the absence of magazine advertising, direct mail could be used to start a new venture, but as pointed out earlier, this method of selling is not the best one to use unless you have a good working knowledge of it beforehand.

Incidentally, much ado about nothing has been made over the terms "mail order" and "direct mail." Direct mail people are quick to claim that they are in the direct mail business, *not* the mail order business. Others claim that the only simon pure mail order is the kind wherein the order is received directly from the ad, and that—in agreement with direct mailers—direct mail is something altogether different. If you like to indulge in such semantic hair-splitting, you can find plenty of conversation among others in the business. For all practical purposes, we can dismiss the subject forthwith by saying that mail order is an all-inclusive term comprising all the various methods of getting business through the mail, and that direct mail is a name for one of those various methods.

Magazine ads are of two main types: *display* ads and *classified* ads. A classified ad is set in straight type, with no illustrations or decorative matter, and appears in long columns with many other similar-appearing ads, all of which are classified according to various headings, such as "Business Opportunities" and "Help Wanted."

A display ad is, in effect, a miniature billboard. It can be, and usually is, dramatized with artwork, photographs, and eye-catching gimmicks of all kinds. The type matter itself may be specially selected to enhance the nature of your message. And, too, a display ad is more likely to be placed in a position in the magazine where it will get the greatest amount of reader attention.

Another distinction between classified and display ads is in the way you normally pay for the space used. In buying classifieds, you pay so much for each word in the ad, or so much for each five-word group. In buying display ads, you pay a certain rate per line or per inch. The display "line" does not mean a line of words. It is a unit of depth and has nothing to do with the number of words in the ad. In a column inch of display space (one column wide) there are fourteen lines. So if a magazine you plan to advertise in says its rate is so much per line, you multiply this by fourteen to find out how much an inch of space will cost you.

There are many things to be said about magazine ads, not all of which will be said in this chapter. One of the generalities we can set forth, however, is that if you plan to sell an item directly from the ad (with no follow-up), you will need to use display space, except in rare instances. If, on the other hand, you are merely seeking a flow of inquiries which you intend to follow up with additional literature, you can usually get them with fairly small amounts of classified space.

About the most important thing we can say about magazine ads is that they must be repeated if their full effect is to be felt. This is perhaps the hardest thing to get across to a novice advertiser. That few of them understand and appreciate the effect of repetition in advertising is evidenced by the great number of one-time advertisers in mail order, who buy just one ad, in the hope that it will somehow produce a tremendous volume of orders, and then quietly disappear from the mail order scene. This is a delusion. It doesn't work that way, except maybe once in ten thousand tries.

Repetition in mail order advertising—as in any other advertising—is a powerful force for success, provided, of course, that the ad to be repeated is a good ad featuring a good product in a good medium.

There is no hard-and-fast rule about how much the returns from an ad will build up (or "pile up") under the impetus of consistent repetition. This varies a great deal from one offer to another. However, it is not unusual for the third insertion of an ad to pull three or four times as much business as did the first insertion. And each consecutive insertion continues to increase the build-up until the maximum pull is reached (which may be at the sixth or twenty-sixth insertion). Once the maximum pull is reached, repetition will keep it at that level until you have skimmed the cream and it is time to try something else. But even after you have withdrawn such an offer, don't throw it away. Keep it in the files; chances are good you can start it again in two or three years and find that it pulls as freshly and profitably as it did the first time around.

There are several good reasons why an ad works better the longer it runs. The build-up is due partly to the fact that the first time an ad appears, it is seen by comparatively few readers. (We're speaking of the typical small-space mail order ad, not the full page blockbuster.) Each time the ad is repeated, it is seen by an increasing number of readers. Another reason is that a lot of mail order buyers, as a matter of policy, do not answer an ad the first time it appears. They wait to see if it appears again next month. If it continues to appear in consecutive or periodic issues of the magazine, then they assume it to be a legitimate offer by a reliable firm and take action.

Then there are many readers who see an ad that interests them and make a mental note to answer it "in a few days." But sure enough, they simply forget it, or the magazine becomes misplaced, or they find they don't have the money at that moment. But next month when they buy a new copy of the magazine and see the ad again, they sit down and send you an order.

An additional factor in the build-up of returns is that magazines are often collected by subscribers and saved indefinitely. Many homes have collections going back for years. These are occasionaly referred to and reread, and the old ad gets another crack at making a sale. Most veteran mail order operators can cite instances in which they received orders from ads published several years previously.

Because of the factors just described, a successful mail order ad in a mass-circulation magazine can be repeated indefinitely without changing the ad's copy, size or appearance. If you can find a complete collection of *Popular Mechanics, Outdoor Life,* or some of the other workhorses of mail order, you might check back and note how many different ads have been running for years without change.

There is one other important factor that makes constant repetition possible. This is the phenomenon of reader flux; that is, a steady change in the magazine's readership from month to month and year to year. One authority refers to this flux as a parade, in which you, as an advertiser, are constantly viewing a passing throng of people, but you never see the same group of paraders for very long at a time. To put it more understandably, perhaps, a magazine is continuously adding new readers and dropping old ones. Therefore, each new issue is read by a somewhat different group of people. Some of last month's readers will have died; others will have cancelled their subscriptions; some will have moved away. In the meantime, new readers have entered their subscriptions and started buying on the newsstands, and you have these as brand new prospects.

It is true that the bulk of a magazine's readership remains fairly constant, but over a period of time it will reveal a definite pattern of turnover. No figures are available on how long it takes a readership to turn over, but possibly seven to ten years would be a good guess. The significance of this turnover is important to you, as a future mail order advertiser, because it makes it possible to run the same ad indefinitely without change. Thus, your ad never gets stale, never saturates the market, because the market is itself in a state of change, and the ad is always new to a new reader. For example, if a magazine has a circulation of 700,000 copies, and its turnover period is seven years, this means that during each year you have 100,-000 new readers who have not seen your ad before.

Most newcomers to mail order are tempted to buy ads in an indiscriminate fashion, partly out of confusion and partly out of the belief that spreading their ads around will hasten their success. If you are facing such a temptation, try to resist it. On the basis of what you already know about mail order, and what you have been told about ads, you can see that it would be wiser to buy several consecutive insertions of an ad in one good magazine than to buy an ad in several different magazines for just one insertion. An ad that appears six succeeding times in one proven magazine will nearly always pull more business than the same ad run once in six different magazines.

After you get your offer worked out and tested, you will, in all probability, want to use as many magazines as you can in order to increase your over-all volume. But don't add new magazines at the expense of old ones. If you have to stop one ad to start another in a different magazine, then you should have more capital. Add new magazines, but don't add them until you can afford them in addition to the ones you're already using.

Chapter 13

Choosing a Magazine to Advertise In

Let's suppose that you now have a product (or service) which you think will sell by mail. Let's suppose further that you believe it will sell directly from the ad. And let's go a step further and assume that you have an ad already written which looks like it will really bring home the bacon. Where do you run the ad?

If these three suppositions were true, you undoubtedly would already have a good idea of where to run the ad. But since this is a hypothetical case, based on a nonexistent product, we can constructively speculate on where the ad should be published.

In determining where to place the ad, we must first ask ourselves some questions about the product itself. To whom does it appeal? Men? Women? Or both? Would it be wanted by sophisticated city-dwellers or by simple rural folk? Is it primarily a gift item or does it serve some instructive or utility purpose? Is it used in the home? The car? The shop? Is it meant primarily for some particular group of tradesmen or professional people—such as chiropractors? Is its principal appeal one of price, or novelty, or distinctiveness?

These are some of the questions you should ask

yourself when you start to advertise a product for sale. In the answers you get will lie the solution to the question "Which magazine should I advertise in?"

Let's say our mythical product is a new type of fishing lure. There certainly wouldn't be any problem in determining the medium to be used for this product. You'd use the outdoors magazines, of course, such as *Outdoor Life, Field and Stream,* and *Sports Afield.* (The order of listing does not imply any superiority of one over another.)

Or, let's say your product is a bargain package of needles and thread. (Don't sneer. Just such an offer became a tremendous mail order success not too long ago.) Again, there would be no problem. You would use the magazines which are read by women who stay at home: *Ladies Home Journal, Family Circle,* and others. You would not use a magazine read primarily by career women—women to whom home chores are secondary to their jobs. Women of this kind do very little of their own sewing.

Again, suppose your product was a purely masculine product, such as a line of unusual pipes. The nature of the product would again dictate the medium to use: magazines that are read by men, men who have the leisure and temperament to be pipe smokers. These would be men in an above-average income bracket, as a rule. Which magazine reaches this type of male? There are several: *True, Argosy, Esquire, Playboy,* and the outdoors magazines listed earlier. There are also the detective magazines, *True Police Cases, True Detective,* and *Police Gazette,* among others.

If the product is a utility item for the home or

garden, say a set of reflective house numbers or a new kind of weeding tool, your medium would be in the home-service or shelter publications, such as *House Beautiful, House & Garden,* and *Better Homes & Gardens.*

If the product appeals primarily to some trade, business, or professional group, you would not use the general consumer magazines at all, but rather one or more of the trade journals going directly and exclusively to people in that particular field. Should you take on a line of imported watchbands, for example, and want to use the mail order method to wholesale them to jewelers, you would advertise in one of the jewelry trade journals, such as *Jewelers' Circular-Keystone.* If you have an item in the office-supply field, and you want to reach retail dealers with it, there is the trade journal for that field known as *Geyer's Topics.*

Should you formulate and package a line of cheap cosmetics or perfumes, you could get to your market easily enough through the magazines that reach the women who buy products of this kind—the romance group, the confessions group, and the movie magazines. There are dozens of different titles on the newsstands in all three groups.

For business plans, self-help books, utility gadgets for the shop, and any other items that appeal to the "doers" and "learners," your media would be the mechanics, vocational, and hobby magazines listed in a previous chapter.

If you have a specialty product that you want other salesmen to sell for you, and there is enough profit in it to pay your salesmen a healthy commission and still have some left for yourself, the place to advertise is in the pages of the specialty-selling magazines, *Opportunity,* and *Specialty Salesman.* Both are very productive pullers for a product with merit.

These illustrations should be sufficient to indicate that the magazine you use to advertise your product in is the magazine which fits the product and the people who are logical prospects for it. You wouldn't advertise a line of cheap perfumes in the outdoor magazines, or fishing lure in the true confessions. Nor would you advertise a set of screwdrivers in *Women's Wear Daily,* or a line of tulip bulbs in *Hardware Age.*

There are many times when your product will be on the borderline, hard to define in terms of exact prospect identity. Take cigarette lighters. Who buys most of them—men or women? Are they bought primarily to use or to give on special occasions? You can't really tell, short of an actual market survey. But surveys are expensive. So the only course open is to use your own judgment plus trial-and-error.

In selecting any medium for advertising your mail order product, there are several important considerations other than the question of whether it fits. One of these is, "Is the magazine I am about to use a 'mail order' magazine?" If you have had much experience with magazines, even as a reader, you will have noticed that some magazines are replete with mail order ads, and that others carry none. There is no easy accounting for this. Why doesn't *The Saturday Evening Post* carry mail order ads? It ought to, in view of its circulation and the type of people it reaches, but it doesn't.

On the other hand, *Better Homes & Gardens* is a superb mail order medium for dozens of different offers. Why is it so much more widely used than *The Saturday Evening Post?* No one knows for sure.

But you don't have to know the "why" of it if you are aware of the curious fact that some magazines are natural mail order mediums and others are not. Your main concern will be in recognizing those which are.

The fact that a magazine is loaded to the brim with mail order ads is irrefutable evidence that that magazine is a good mail order medium. It is that magazine in which you want to advertise. Don't believe the popular fallacy that since a magazine already has so many ads running in it, yours would merely be lost in the shuffle. In point of fact, the reverse is true.

Your ad stands a better chance of paying off when it is placed in proximity to other mail order ads, even though there may be dozens of others surrounding it. Glance at the mail order columns in *Popular Mechanics.* There you see literally hundreds of small ads jammed up tightly against one another—page after page of them. "Who on earth," you ask yourself, "would read my little ad if it were buried among a thousand others?" Plenty of people. One firm recently ran a $10 classified ad in one of the mechanics magazines, and the first insertion of it pulled a thousand inquiries. Had the same ad been placed in a magazine not having many similar mail order ads, it is doubtful that the ad would have been anywhere near as productive as it was.

Another of the important considerations in selecting

a medium is to use the one which gives you the most readers per ad dollar. This is where the newcomer often errs, believing that the lowest-cost publication is the cheapest to buy. The reverse is usually true. A simple illustration will prove this: Is it cheaper to pay twenty-five cents per word for an ad in a magazine which has 200,000 readers, or seventy-five cents a word in one which has a million readers? You don't need a slide rule to work that one out. The seventy-five-cent-per-word medium is the cheaper, even though it calls for a larger cash outlay. That's because you get five times as many readers for only three times the cost. In the first instance, a penny per word buys eight thousand readers. In the second, a penny buys thirteen thousand.

Whenever you select a potential ad medium, put it to the test just outlined. Don't think in terms of how many dollars are involved, but only in terms of how many readers you get per dollar—or per penny. Then buy the one that gives you the most for your dollar or penny.

You may recall that in an earlier chapter we stated that, reader for reader, newspapers are very expensive to use for mail order advertising. That is because newspapers, as a whole, cost an excessive amount per reader when measured against magazines. With the possible exception of the metropolitan papers with national Sunday editions, you pay much more for newspaper ads than you do for national magazine ads. The most expensive newspaper space of all is in the small town daily or weekly. Consider the *Dry Gulch Gazette,* for example. It has a circulation of ten thousand. A classified ad in it cost twelve cents per word. To get some idea of how high this rate actually is, assume that the circulation of this paper suddenly went to a million and the ad rate went up proportionately. You would then be paying $12 per word for the same ad! The best classified media in the country cost only about one-tenth as much.

The practice of buying the most readers for each ad dollar is especially important when you are using classified ads only. Whereas a display ad might pay out in a low-circulation, high-reader-cost medium, a classified almost never will, particularly if it asks for any kind of remittance. Further, a classified ad is greatly handicapped by its inconspicuousness and lack of attention-getting devices. To overcome its handicaps, a classified must be placed where it is exposed to great numbers of readers. The mechanics magazines, as well as some of the mass-circulation detective magazines and metropolitan newspapers, make it possible for the small-budget advertiser to put his message where the odds are very much in his favor. Readership of at least two of the mechanics magazines is around the five million mark, and you can buy classifieds in these publications for a comparatively low amount, about $1.25 per word.

The usefulness of the classified ad is quite limited except as a means of pulling inquiries. As an inquiry-getter, it can and often does work extremely well. If your subsequent sale is sufficiently large, the cost of getting the inquiry through classifieds is negligible. If we were forced to prescribe the best all-around method of making mail sales that a beginner could start with,

it would be the inquiry follow-up method, using classified ads to pull inquiries and good follow-up letters to
close the sales. But, as qualified earlier, the use of
this method depends on what you are selling.

This book won't go into the details of making up a
classified ad, except to point out that you should avoid
asking your reader for a remittance of any kind. To
do so will greatly reduce the number of inquiries you
receive, and the dimes and quarters that many such
ads ask for do not begin to cover your ad costs except
in rare cases. If you are prepared to follow up your
inquiries with good sales literature, by all means offer
"complete information free." Why should an inquirer
send you a dime to find out what it is you have for
sale?

There is one exception to the above remarks. That
is when you are using a "leader" as a means of pre-
selecting your prospects to prepare them for a much
larger sale. A leader, in mail order parlance, is an
item that has value in itself but is used to get high-
grade inquiries and weed out curiosity seekers. It
usually sells for a very small sum, perhaps ten cents or
a quarter—rarely more—and is directly related to an
item of much larger price which you hope to sell to
the leader buyer.

For example, if you are offering a book of business
plans for $5, you might single out one or two of the
better plans, put them into a separate folio or booklet,
and offer them as a leader, through classified ads, for
twenty-five cents. Then, to the persons who order the
twenty-five-cent leader booklet, you send the follow-up
mailing offering the complete book of plans for $5.

The same leader principle can be adapted to nearly any kind of offer, and is a very productive and dependable method of selling by mail.

Perhaps the best advice you can get about preparing and inserting classified ads has been ably and succinctly stated by F. W. Johnson, classified ad manager at *Popular Mechanics* magazine. His little booklet, *Profits from Classified Advertising,* is something of a minor classic in its field, and you should get a copy and study it thoroughly.

Chapter 14

When to Run Your Magazine Ads

Mail order, like most other fields of business, has certain seasonal characteristics. There are seasons when some mail order products sell like wildfire, and others when they are completely dormant.

For the general run of mail order offers, late fall is the time when sales begin to flow heavily, and they increase steadily through midwinter. They continue at a good rate through winter and early spring, and then subside quickly. Through early and middle summer activity is at a lull.

As a mail order operator you will want to take advantage of this rise and fall of sales activity, capitalizing on the peak months by doing your heaviest advertising during them.

How the seasons will affect your particular product depends entirely on the product, of course, so you should take the above remarks subject to qualification.

The seasonal aspect of mail order is not inconsistent with what was stated earlier about ad repetition. It only means that after discovering the length of the season for your product, you be repetitious within the season. You would not want to repeat an ad during the off-season just to satisfy the need for repetition, but you can and should repeat your ads as often as possible during the eight or nine months of the normal mail order season. Also, after finding out which of the season's months are your peak months, you will find it profitable to run extra ads during those months.

Products vary a great deal in the extent to which they are affected by the seasons. Items which are designed and sold primarily as gifts sell best during November and the first two weeks in December. (Orders that come in later than that cannot usually be filled and returned to the customer by Christmas Day.) If you were to handle such gift items, you would want to place your heaviest advertising in the November and December issues of the chosen media. (*Note:* December issues are usually in readers' hands by the fifth of December, to give them time to make their Christmas purchases and assure them of pre-Christmas delivery.)

On the other hand, if you were selling fishing gear, your best advertising season would begin in February and run through June. If you handled garden tools or other items for outdoor living, your season would begin in early spring and end in midsummer, with perhaps an additional spurt of sales activity in the early fall.

There are some products which are affected by the seasons to only a minor degree. Products in the business-service field, for example, often enjoy steady year-round sales, with the summer making only a slight ripple in the sales volume. Such items as office supplies, specialty printing, collection aids, and other business services usually suffer very little seasonal diminution.

Similarly, books and plans on money-making subjects do not undergo such an extréme ebb and flow of sales as do gift items and other consumer products. Most firms that sell plans on how to make money keep their advertising programs going full blast from January through December. The same is true of correspondence schools.

Books designed to entertain rather than instruct sell slowly during the warm months but pick up speed rapidly as winter approaches. This is true whether they are sold by direct mail or direct from ads. Self-help books are not so seriously affected.

If you are on the mailing lists of any of the book clubs or popular magazines, you probably have noticed that you receive most of their sales letters and other promotional efforts during November, December, and January. If you are on the mailing lists of companies selling books and courses of a how-to nature, you are likely to receive their offers any time of the year.

In the final analysis, there is only one way to find out what the seasonal characteristics of a specific product are, and that way is to *test.* The foregoing information is meant to serve as a general guide line, but it will not replace the testing that you eventually will have to do.

Remember, your mail order career will be one of endless testing. Testing for product, testing for method, testing for medium, and now, testing for season. There is no way you can avoid testing in mail order. About the best you can do is to narrow the odds against you by intelligent analysis beforehand, prior to the actual tests, but this merely reduces the risk—it doesn't eliminate the necessity for testing.

Chapter 15

How to Change an Inquiry into a Sale

If you have ever done any personal selling, you know how difficult it is to go out with your sample case under your arm, stop the first likely-looking prospect you run into, and try to interest him in your offer. Chances are that such a "cold" prospect would brush you off forthwith, or at best, start showing you the door about thirty seconds after you had said hello.

But, on the other hand, if you're sitting at home in the evening and a stranger comes to your door and says, "Say, I heard you were selling a line of Widgetts, and I'd like to look them over," your chances of selling this "hot" prospect are extremely good.

The difference between calling on a cold prospect and having a hot prospect call on you is the difference between selling direct from the ad and selling by inquiry follow-up. When you use the inquiry follow-up method, you deal with relatively hot prospects. Inquirers are prewarmed prospects, and they have come to you with their minds already open to receive the details of your offer. Whether they buy or not depends entirely on you and the power of your sales literature.

It's no feat of magic to get inquiries. Offer free information on any worthwhile product or offer, and you'll get barrels of inquiries, provided your ad makes the offer sound interesting enough. But changing these inquiries into sales requires a good deal of selling legerdemain.

To convert a satisfactory number of inquiries into sales requires that you not only have a good product at a fair price, but—most important—the kind of follow-up material that makes your prospect want to buy it.

Most inquiry follow-ups use the standard format outlined in a preceding chapter; i.e., sales letter, circular, order form, and reply envelope. If you follow this format for a majority of products, you won't usually go wrong. (There are many other formats and follow-up devices, but these *exotica* are developed and used by firms with years of mail selling experience.)

Second in importance to the standard follow-up format is the old mail order stand-by, the booklet. This is particularly useful in selling items in the higher-price bracket or items that require a lot of explanation.

One man started out selling a product of his own manufacture using the standard format. It worked very well, resulting in the conversion of about twenty percent of his inquiries into sales. After using this technique awhile, he discovered that there was one dominant element in his sales literature that was mainly responsible for the closing of his sales. Written into his sales letter was a brief dramatic episode in which he narrated the experience of a user in an extremely interesting manner. After learning that it was this paragraph that was doing the most to stimulate sales, he decided that if a little was good, a lot would be even better. So he had his ad agency prepare a new follow-up piece—a thirty-six-page booklet—which dramatized every aspect of the product just as he had been doing in the sales letter. The booklet was one long-running narrative about the product: how it was conceived, how it was tested and proved in the field, how it met with instant success among users, and the reports users had sent in after trying it, as well as a biography of the man who had invented the product to begin with.

A test mailing was made of the booklet, in place of the standard follow-up, and the percentage of sales conversion rose from twenty percent to approximately forty percent. The old follow-up was then scrapped.

This is an unusual, and irregular, instance, but it worked. In the first place, the booklet violated several mail order principles or at least gave them a terrific warping. Instead of dealing in terms of what the product would do for the customer, it took him on a written tour of the product's history and development . . . but this history was so dramatized that it was continuously interesting, and apparently gave the prospect a chance to identify with the man who had originated and sold the idea. By the time the prospect got to the last page of the booklet, he was completely sold, however indirectly the job had been done.

The elements of your follow-up should be as good as you and your ad writer know how to make them. In this connection, don't attempt to write and lay out your own follow-up pieces unless you have had a great deal of mail order experience. It is far less expensive in the long run to have a professional do it for you. (You can find the names and addresses of these people in the mail order trade journals, such as *Reporter of Direct Mail Advertising* and *Progressive Mail Trade*. See back of book for addresses.)

If you have had no experience in writing advertising copy, it won't pay you to experiment at the expense of sales. Bad copy can cost you thousands of dollars a year in business you *didn't* get. The difference between bad copy and good copy is very great, although hard to discern beforehand. One particular individual might not be able to see any difference, but the difference will show up drastically when you place the ad in front of thousands of readers of a magazine. A good ad writer knows that on some people who read it, his copy will make no impression whatever. He also knows that his copy will have the opposite effect on a profitable number of readers, and that is the result you are both shooting for.

If you must develop your own follow-up material, however, there is one sure way to do it with the least amount of creative struggle and sales risk. The method works as follows: Having decided what you are going to sell by the inquiry follow-up technique, you search several magazines until you find another firm that is already selling a product similar in nature to yours. Then you determine whether this firm is successful or not by finding out how long it has been advertising and using its present follow-up material.

Your next step is to send an inquiry to this firm asking for free literature. Having it at hand, you study it, analyze it, and parallel it in terms of your own product. Be careful not to pirate, or plagiarize, anything belonging to the other firm. But paralleling is permissible. It's done all the time, even by professionals who don't need to take this kind of short cut. About the only things that are not freely paralleled and imitated are patented and copyrighted items, trademarks, and things so protected.

You can learn a great deal about developing follow-ups by using the parallel procedure just described. If possible, try to locate not just one but several firms selling products similar to yours, and take a look at their literature, also. From a variety of such literature, you can soon deduce the similarities that are common to all and pinpoint those specific features which you need to parallel in your own material.

Aside from having the best possible sales copy in your follow-up mailing, there are several additional things you can do to stimulate your sales to inquirers. One of the most important is to answer an inquiry as soon as possible after you receive it. Don't wait a day or two; certainly you wouldn't wait a week or more before sending the information your prospect asked for. Remember, he was warmed up at the time he sent his card or letter requesting more information, and he will remain warm just long enough for your letter to reach him by return mail. If he has to wait longer, he starts to cool rapidly. He becomes annoyed and offended that you care so little about him as to delay your response. He soon adopts the attitude that if you are not interested in making a sale to him, he is most certainly not interested in buying your product.

Another important point, touched on earlier in the book, is to make it easy for your prospect to order. Always include an order form and reply envelope (preferably the business-reply kind) in your mailings.

Keep the order form as simple and explicit as you can. Leave plenty of room for your buyer to write in his name and address, and indicate where to do so. Suggest that he print the information. (Mail order customers have notoriously bad handwriting.) Have spaces for entering the amount of money he is remitting with the order, and the form it takes—whether cash, money order, or check. Bear in mind that he is sending his own money away, and he wants to feel as secure as possible about doing it. Don't ask him to pay his own postage. The lack of a stamp has been the death of many a sale.

The use of a business-reply envelope can boost your percentage of sales five percent or more. Think what this would mean on the basis of a thousand inquiries. If you normally close twenty percent of them, an extra five percent would be ten extra orders— at no extra sales cost.

In connection with follow-ups, you probably have wondered what is the "average" percentage of sales closed to a given number of inquiries. There is no definite answer to this. Some firms feel they are doing well if they convert ten percent of their inquiries into sales. Others are happy with five percent. Still others need fifteen percent to break even. There have been cases of firms closing fifty percent or more of their inquiries, but these are the exceptions by far. The only thing you have to be concerned with is converting enough of the inquiries to yield you a worthwhile profit over and above your product, advertising, and follow-up costs.

Chapter 16

When and How to Use Direct Mail

Direct mail is used in many ways. New mothers use it to announce births. Charities use it to solicit money. Creditors use it to send bills. Debtors use it to send excuses. Lovers use it to exchange romantic notes. And politicians use it to stir up votes.

But mail order people use it to make money.

You, too, can make money by direct mail by meeting three or four conditions. One, you have to have something good to sell. Two, you have to have a mailing piece that will sell it. Three, you have to have the names and addresses of the people who are prospects for it. And, four, you have to have a lot of these names and addresses.

Direct mail is that simple—or that complicated. If you're experienced with it, you know it is that complicated. If it looks that simple to you, you may approach it with complete self-assurance and faith and proceed to make a fortune. It has been done, and in all probability will be done again.

Getting into direct mail is easy. You locate a product or service having the mail order characteristics previously mentioned. After studying it awhile, you conclude that it would not be suitable for direct-from-

ad or inquiry follow-up selling. So you decide that
direct mail is the logical method.

Having made this decision, you will roughly follow
the procedure that has been followed countless of
times by hundreds of direct-mail sellers. Probably the
first thing you'll do is sit down at the typewriter and
write a sales letter. (This may not be the first thing
you do, but it's as good a place to start as any.) Now
if you deliberately sit down at the typewriter to compose a sales letter, you will probably write a stinkeroo
that wouldn't sell rifles to revolutionists.

But if, on the other hand, you forget all the for-
midable and formal rules you have ever read about
writing sales letters, and instead, sit down and write
a polite, well-reasoned letter to a specific person asking
him to buy your product, you will probably end up
with a gem of a selling letter. If, in attempting to
write the letter yourself, you sit and squirm self-con-
sciously at the typewriter without getting anything
concrete down on paper, then the best thing for you
to do is to forget about writing the letter yourself and
turn it over to a professional sales-letter writer. There
are some good ones scattered around the country who
will charge you a modest fee for their services, but
their work will be well worth it.

However, if you're a persistent cuss, you'll write
that sales letter if it kills you. Such tenacity deserves
an assist, and here's one in the form of a suggestion:
When you start to write your sales letter, go to the
family album and take out a picture of one of your
relatives—one who is of the same sex and economic
circumstances as the typical prospect for your offer—

and tack this picture to the wall behind your typewriter, where you can see it as you type. If you don't
like your relatives, just search the newspaper for a
photograph of someone who represents your mental
image of your prospect. Having put the picture up
on the wall where it can be seen, begin your letter
and write it as a *personal* one to the character you see
in the picture. Forget all about people; instead, write
your letter to this one particular person. By this procedure you will almost always write a better letter—
one that is convincing and sincere, as well as
enthusiastic.

Now in writing the letter to sell your product, it
will occur to you as you go along from paragraph to
paragraph that there are many things you can tell the
prospect, but if you try to tell them all in this letter,
it will be far too long to read. So it dawns on you that
many of the things that should be said can be left out
of the letter and put on a separate piece of paper. After
all, you're writing what amounts to a personal letter,
and you don't want to bore your reader with too many
details—but you don't want to leave them out either.
So you collect all these extra details and bits of information about the product and put them in "circular"
form, to be mailed along with your letter. It also
occurs to you that your prospect might be interested
in a picture of the product, so you plan on putting
it in the circular, too.

At this point, you are working on two different
things at once: a sales letter and a circular. Unless
you are unusual, you will probably be a bit confused
as to which things go into which of the two pieces.

When and How to Use Direct Mail

Here is a simple rule of thumb: In the letter you tell your prospect what your product *does* (for him). In the circular you tell him what your product *is*. In the letter you talk benefits and advantages. In the circular, you describe physical features and characteristics.

Assuming that you have now written your letter and circular, and are secretly pleased with your handiwork, the next step in your direct-mail procedure is to go to a printer. You do this because you want these pieces produced in quantity. It occurred to you as you were typing that you were typing only *one* letter to *one* prospect, and if you sent just this one letter out, that particular prospect might not want to buy. So you said to yourself, "Instead of sending just one letter, I'll send a thousand. Out of that many, somebody is sure to buy my product!"

So you take your typewritten copy to a printer and tell him to make you a thousand of each one—letter and circular. And since the letter is a more or less personal one, even though it is to be mailed to a thousand people, you tell him to make it look as much like a typewritten letter as possible. The circular can be printed in the regular way. (*Note*: There are several different processes for turning out sales letters that look as much like individually typed letters as possible. The best—and most expensive—is autotyping, which usually is prohibitive in cost for mass mailings. In terms of looks and cost the two best ones are Multigraphing and photo-offsetting. Your printer can explain the difference.)

While you're at the printer's, you also order a thousand envelopes to mail your letter and circular out in, and a thousand reply envelopes to get the orders back in. (Nope, you won't get a thousand orders back, but you have to send out that many reply envelopes.) You also have him print you a thousand order forms.

A few days later the printer calls you and says your stuff is ready. You rush eagerly to pick it up, and carry the bundles back to your home or office. Spreading the various pieces out on the floor or a large table, you start to collate them. Collating simply means taking one of each of the pieces that go into the envelope and inserting them into it. About midnight you will have gotten all the letters, circulars, etc. into the envelopes, sealed them, put stamps on them, and will be ready to take them to the post office. Bright and early the next morning you do just that.

About four days later the suspense has become unbearable. You have watched for the postman day after day, and each delivery has brought no orders in the familiar reply envelopes. Then, on the fifth day, you get an order—and you're walking around on Cloud Nine. The next day five orders come in, and you know you've struck it rich. But then the next day . . . and the next . . . and the next . . . nothing happens. Two weeks later a couple of orders come straggling in, but by then your disappointment is so great that they no longer give you joy.

It's incredible. You mailed a thousand letters and got only eight orders. How could that be possible? You simply can't imagine what went wrong, but if you're made out of good mail order stuff, you'll jolly well set about finding out!

It is at this point that you really begin to understand direct mail. You can read all the books in the library on the subject, and they won't mean as much to you as the experience we've just described. (Strictly a hypothetical example, oversimplified to give you a quick capsule sketch of a typical beginner's entree into direct mailing.) Direct mail is like swimming or piloting an airplane: You can't fully learn it without actually jumping in and doing it. This is no argument against reading books on the subject. By all means do so; the more the merrier. But don't expect the books to take the place of a good dose of experience; on the contrary, it is usually after you've gotten your feet good and wet that the books begin to make sense and become of real help. Because by then you can relate what you read to your own tangible experience.

There is only one way to get into direct mail, and that way is to hit on a product or service that looks good (in terms of the previously listed mail order requirements), and roughly following the procedure outlined in this chapter, give it a test. The test mailing will give you a feel of direct mail and will help you decide in which direction to go beyond that. If the test is successful, then you continue mailing at the same or an increased rate; if it fails, you look for another offer and try again.

You'd be perfectly justified in saying that the preceding capsule version of the direct-mail business is not a particularly appetizing or encouraging one, not at all the kind of thing you're used to reading and hearing about. If it sounds that way to you, please understand that our purpose in so presenting it has been to impress upon you the fact that direct mail does involve a high element of risk, especially at the start, and unless you are willing and able to afford the risk, it might be wise for you to use one of the other two methods in the beginning.

There is an optimistic side, however. That is that a great deal of money is being made by many different firms who operate strictly by direct mail, and the odds are even that if you try long enough, hard enough, and intelligently enough, you can be one of them.

For the newcomer, direct mail should serve primarily as an adjunct to direct-from-ad or inquiry follow-up selling. If you sell from ads, you can test direct mail, on a small scale, as you go along, being careful not to let it siphon off funds that you need for the normal operation of your direct-from-ad business. It is easy to acquire some name lists from outside sources and send your mailing pieces to these prospects. Should small-scale tests then indicate that direct mail is your most profitable method of doing business, you could wisely drop the other methods and devote all your efforts to this one.

Numerous products lend themselves to profitable direct-mail selling. Current direct-mail sellers are office equipment, self-help books, collection forms, standardized business forms, low-cost insurance, newsletters, business cards, duplicating machines,, medical books, war histories, business books, neckties, advertising specialties, record players, steel shelving, trees and nursery items, and dozens of others. (If you are not now receiving a good many direct-mail offers, it will pay you to get your name on some lists and start receiving them.)

In anything that is successfully sold by direct mail,

there will always be certain peculiar characteristics. One of these is the average unit of sale. It almost never will be under $5. It is next to impossible to sell anything by direct mail for less than this amount and make a profit. This fact is attributable primarily to the high costs of printing, postage, and labor—all of which have a steady trend upward. So as you go about selecting something to offer by this method, bear the price consideration in mind. Keep it at $5 or more. The ideal price for a direct-mail item is probably $10 or slightly below.

Another outstanding quality of successful direct-mail offers is uniqueness. Examine a dozen different propositions, and you will find that there will be something definitely unique about each one. The product itself may not be unique, but it will have unique features of function or design. Or it may be a run-of-the-mill product which carries a uniquely attractive price. Or, in another instance, it may be a standard product which carries with it a unique premium offer. But in all cases, whatever the product, the offer will have something unique or different about it to distinguish it from other direct-mail offers and to differentiate it from similar goods sold in stores.

A third quality of a good direct-mail proposition is that it be something which is used up, worn out, or otherwise leads to another sale in the future. As in selling direct from the ad, you cannot thrive in direct mail on customers who buy just one time. You must sell to them a second time, and keep on selling to them, whether you sell them more of the same item or something that is different yet related to the first item. Ideally, the first order is used up by the customer quickly, and he sends in an order for more of the same without further solicitation or sales cost. Thus, the second order contains a long, clean profit, unburdened by any further mailing or effort outside of filling the order. This kind of repeat potential is present in all successful direct-mail sellers. If the product you select is not in itself susceptible to being used up, then you must look around for a similar item that you can sell to the people who buy the first one. For example, a firm that sells a duplicating machine generates its repeat business through the sale of duplicating paper, ink, and other supplies. If it were to sell the machine only, it would not have a very profitable operation.

In direct mail your profit almost never will be in making that first sale but in making subsequent sales. The profit is there to be made after you have built up a good list of customers, because it is much easier to sell to them the second time. For instance, a firm dealing in printed forms realizes about a two percent return from its first "cold mailing" to businessmen. Out of a million letters mailed, the firm accumulates twenty thousand customers. A lot of customers, but not very much profit. But this firms then sends out a mailing to these customers after an interval, and realizes nearly a ten percent response. In the ten percent response, there is a very substantial profit; in fact, the profit from mailing to their twenty thousand customers is greater than their profit in mailing one million cold letters.

Another feature of a good direct-mail offer is that it rarely ever asks for a remittance in advance. It has been found that the number of orders received from a mailing can be increased considerably by offering to ship on approval or on open account. It has also been found that while shipping on such terms can raise the response a great deal, the credit loss is not raised proportionately. Most people, it is true, are honest. If they receive a satisfactory product which lives up to its original advertising claims, they will pay for it. Naturally, you will run into some professional dead beats who won't pay for the goods, but these are in the minority and a small price to pay for the large increase in volume of orders you can usually expect by offering to ship on approval or credit. (It is taken for granted, of course, that you would pre-select your prospects by financial or economic standing in order to make certain that they have the money to buy what you have to offer. Mailing-list counselors can be invaluable in helping you select lists of prospects who are financially responsible.)

These, then, are the main characteristics of a good direct-mail offer: a price of $5 or more, repeat potential, uniqueness of product or offer, and liberal selling terms. That a product embodies all these features does not guarantee its success, of course. Other matters will have their effect also: the quality of the lists you use, the impressiveness of your mailing, the season and timing. But it can safely be said that if an offer does *not* possess these main characteristics, it is not likely to sell profitably by direct mail.

In discussing the qualities of a direct-mail product, no mention was made of two other important features which by now should be an integral part of your mail order thinking. One, the product should have a long profit margin, and two, the product must be guaranteed. Most direct-mail products have a profit ranging from fifty to eighty percent. The longer the profit, the better off you are. Don't feel guilty about making a long profit on a worthwhile product. You'll need every bit of your margin to cover your costs, expand your mailings, and yield a profit for yourself.

The matter of guarantees is a special one and will be dealt with in a later chapter. At this point, it suffices to say that you must guarantee your product in mail order and live up to your guarantee. Nothing will help you make sales faster or create more satisfied customers. Nothing will make customers angrier and cause you to lose them faster than not living up to your guarantee.

No discussion of direct mail would be complete without a statement of what you can expect in the way of response to your mailings. There is no definite answer to this, except that it nearly always is less than you think it will be. Some firms get by with fewer orders per thousand letters than others. Magazines, as a rule, can afford to accept a response of one-half to one percent because of their high percentage of renewals in future years. Specialized mailings to special groups of prospects may produce orders to the extent of five percent or so. General consumer mailings rarely exceed a two percent response. A "teaser" mailing, offering a free gift or premium only, may pull as high as forty to fifty percent. In general, if you sell a product in the $5 to $10 range, in which you have a seventy percent profit margin, and you pull two percent in orders, you are doing very well—probably above average.

Chapter 17

How to Write a Sales Letter

The best way to write a sales letter is vicariously—through a professional copywriter. The next best way is to do it yourself.

In mail order you nearly always need one or more sales letters. In inquiry follow-up and direct mail the letter is the soul of your business. It is more important than any piece you send out, although this statement may precipitate some dispute among other mail order people. It is the letter that ultimately sways your prospect for or against your offer and causes him to buy or not to buy.

There is an astounding difference between a good sales letter and a bad one. Although, as in display ads, the difference may be hard to detect in advance, it shows up in a very dramatic way in the number of orders pulled. A good letter often will do five or ten times the business that a poor one does. The only way to find out which is which is by testing.

There are many ways to go about writing a sales letter. Every writer has his own method, his own set of psychic conditions; and don't feel badly if, in sitting down to write your letter, you feel that you haven't made quite the right preliminary motions. It doesn't matter how you approach the task; you can write your letter in longhand or in Sanskrit, while in bed or hanging from the parallel bars. Just so you get it down on paper and it sells.

To write a sales letter to sell a product, you must first have the product. Now if you have the product, or a sample of it, set it on your desk alongside of your typewriter. Next, crank a blank sheet of paper into your typewriter. Then conjure up a mental image of a particular person to whom you think you can sell this particular product. (If your cerebellum screen is a little snowy, turn it off and follow the method given in Chapter XVI: Dig out a picture of a relative and tack it to the wall in front of you.)

Now you have the perfect setting in which to compose a sales letter. You have the prospect in your head or on the wall; you have the product on the desk beside you; and you have the means of communicating the sales message in your typewriter.

All you have to do now is convince the character in your mind that he needs and must have the product on your desk. Whether you succeed or not depends entirely on the words you select and the order in which you line them up.

That is about all anybody can tell you about how to write a sales letter. True, you can buy dozens of books on the subject; you can go to night school and hear lecturers describe various sure-fire techniques; you can take correspondence courses in copywriting. But none of these activities will equip you to write a particular sales letter to sell your particular product. From the moment you hit the first typewriter key, you discover that you are strictly on your own, and all the rules and tricks you've learned will not do the writing for you.

There is, of course, the standard sales formula to which any finished sales letter must conform. It is: *attention, interest, desire,* and *action.* A good letter will contain all the elements of this formula. Take the first one, *attention.* You know beforehand that to get a prospect to read your letter, you must first get his attention. If you don't grab his attention quickly, into the wastebasket goes your letter. So you put something in the letter that will catch his eye, that will stop him from whatever else he is thinking about and cause his mind to focus on what *you* have to say. This "something," normally called the headline, goes at the top of your letter, where it will be seen before the rest of the copy.

Your attention-getter is very important. It must not only get your prospect's attention, but it must lead logically into the main portion of your letter. The best attention-getter is one that grows out of your product and contains your essential sales appeal. Here is a sample from the daily mail. See if it doesn't tie up the particular product with a good attention-getting technique: "Zip through your household chores with this Amazing Power Tool Set in your home for 7 days Free!"

Here's another: "Court Summons! Accidents! Suits! Divorce!" (That string of frightening words is enough to get anybody's attention.) This eye-stopping opener was used to introduce a letter offering a book on law.

Here's another, selling a book on medical matters:

"Do you know the few essentials of information and technique that make men adequate?" Clearly an injection of the sexual element to sell a fairly commonplace book, but very effective.

Those are three attention-getters that are built in, or derived from the product itself. However, you can't always be lucky enough to have such a custom-built opener. In its absence, you can usually rely on one of the stock openers. You've seen many of them in letters you've received in the past. They are identified by such words as "New!" "At Last!" "Now!" "Free!" "You Are Invited To Accept . . ." "You Have Been Referred to Us by a Mutual Acquaintance," and "Have You Heard the News?"

These are a few of the standardized openings you'll find in hundreds of different sales letters. They aren't copyrighted; you can take any one of them and adapt it to fit your letter. You can find many more good attention-getters just by examining the direct-mail offers you get in your daily mail. (In fact, these are the best possible examples you can use, and because they are a common part of every office and household, we have not used space here to reproduce any of them.)

If you aren't receiving any direct-mail offers, by all means, subscribe to a couple of magazines or buy something else by mail that will automatically get your name on some mailing lists. If you get on one or two, you will soon be on a dozen or more and start receiving offers of all kinds. That's because mailing-list houses sell the customer lists of one firm to many other firms.

All good attention-getters embody news, intrigue,

shock, or unusual information. Put any of these elements into your headline and you're bound to get attention. Everybody is interested in something "new." If you have a new product, or one which is new to the prospect, include the news angle in your opener.

Intrigue is good if it is carefully handled. Here's a good example: "Once in a lifetime, a man makes a decision that means more than anything else he ever does . . ." Now *there* is an opener! It would be hard to resist finding out what this "decision" is, impossible to keep from reading the rest of the letter.

Shock is sure to get attention, but it must be the right kind of shock. Not the kind you create by yelling "Fire!" in a crowded theatre. A fine example is the one contained in a letter sent to electronics engineers by a prominent insurance company. It said, "If you died tonight, would your wife be able to operate your slide rule . . ." And then the story led into the need of a man in such a highly specialized occupation to protect those who would not be able to step into his shoes. The letter sold a lot of insurance.

Not only your opener but the entire letter should stress those things which will be of selfish interest to your prospect. You never write your letter around *your* reasons for wanting him to buy your product— instead, you concentrate on *his* reasons for buying it. You don't write to a prospect and say, "Look, Jack, I want you to buy this Widgett because I am trying to get a new car and it will help me if you buy the Widgett." Such a plea might elicit a little sympathy, but it won't get you a new car. Instead, you say, "I want you to buy this Widgett because it will make you more attractive to women . . . help you get a raise . . . make you the envy of the country club set . . ." and so on. See the difference?

In this discussion of the composition of sales letters, it is assumed that you have a passing knowledge of business letters and the usual form they take. If you don't, hunt up a textbook on business correspondence and relearn how to write a business letter. The only difference between a conventional business letter and a direct-mail sales letter is the *purpose*. A sales letter is meant to get orders. With one or two exceptions, the form is the same as that followed by any business letter.

Whereas a business letter opens with the name and address of the person to whom you're writing and includes a salutation, most mail order sales letters nowadays do away with these items completely, because it is not economically feasible in most mass-mailing operations to fill them in.

Just as most sales letters dispense with a formal salutation, they also omit the nauseatingly familiar "Dear Friend" that used to be used so regularly. Many people resent being called "Dear" and "Friend," especially by someone at a remote distance who has no right to presume such a relationship.

The other essential difference between a business letter and a sales letter is the one previously discussed—the attention-getter, headline, opener, or whatever you choose to call it. This usually takes the form of two or three double-spaced typewritten lines (often indented or staggered) above the main body of the letter, where the salutation normally is situated.

There are two general ways to get attention in sales-letter copy. One is to make a statement; the other is to ask a question. If you make a statement, it should contain something that is new, different, or interesting. If you ask a question, ask one which cannot be answered immediately with a Yes or No; or if it does call for a spontaneous answer, be sure the answer is Yes, so as to put the prospect into an affirmative frame of mind for the rest of the message.

Here are several tips on writing effective headlines:

Begin your headline with the word "New" or "Now."
Begin your headline with the words "At Last!"
Begin your headline with "How" or "How To."
Begin your headline with the word "Which."
Talk about money in your headline . . . in dollars and cents.
Use the word "Free."
Use the word "Amazing."

Once you have thought out a suitable headline for your sales letter, one that will get attention from your reader, your next step is to convert this *attention* into *interest*. This is most often done by elaborating or explaining the headline. Here is an example:

THE HEADLINE: DO YOU WANT TO SPEND THE REST OF YOUR LIFE IN THE ATTIC . . . OR ON THE SEASHORE?

Such a headline immediately arouses curiosity, and leads right into the main body of the letter, which goes on to say:

Maybe you wouldn't choose either one, but it's a fact that millions of people are actually beginning to plan what they are going to do with themselves, and we feel you are one of them. An exciting new magazine, ..., dedicated to all the adventure of mature life, is being printed right now . . .

From that point on, the rest is easy. The letter continues to describe the product (in this case, a magazine) in terms which will make the reader want to subscribe to it; in other words, *desire.* And if the desire is fired to the proper temperature, the final element of our formula, *action,* will be forthcoming. Because if you make a person *want* a product more than he wants the money he is being asked to part with, he'll buy it.

There are several ways to go about putting desire-inducing elements into your sales letter. But as in writing the letter, all this instruction can do is provide a method or formula . . . it cannot do the actual work for you.

The best approach is to take a sample of your product and put it on your desk or in some other spot where you can see it, handle it, smell it, measure it, taste it, and weigh it. Then, with pen and paper or typewriter make as comprehensive a list as you possibly can of all the positive qualities of the product, beginning with those you think are most appealing, and ending with the least important ones.

Once you have such a list of qualities or features, you simply proceed to turn each listed quality into a "selling phrase."

Suppose the item is pastel colored. You might turn

this into a selling phrase by saying, "The Gizmo is beautifully finished in tasteful pastel shades, to blend with the modern atmosphere of your home."

Suppose it is made of aluminum—not a very startling fact, but one which under many circumstances could be turned into a selling phrase or sentence by pointing up the sales features of aluminum itself. Here is an example: "Durably constructed of finest aluminum to assure you of long rust-free, break-free life!"

These are prosaic examples, to be sure, but you can see the moral: *Any* quality of *any* product can be skillfully turned into a selling phrase if you work at it a little. (This includes the *bad* qualities!)

Once you have itemized the qualities of your product and turned them into the best selling phrases of which you are capable, your next step is to write your letter in such a manner that it incorporates—in an easy-to-read, fluid sequence—all the phrases you've devised.

If you have done a good job of it up to this point, you have probably succeeded in arousing some degree of desire in your prospect, and the next stage is to solidify this desire by demonstrating that what you have told him is true.

The matter of *proof* is important to an effective sales letter, and should be built into every letter you use. Its most popular form is the testimonial from a satisfied user. (It is no trick to get all the good testimonials you can use; all you need do, after you have sold a number of your products, is write to your customers and ask them to give you their personal opinions and experiences with the product. A surprising number of your customers will be more than glad to do this.)

Other forms of proof are specific statements of value, as supported by manufacturers' literature, research reports, and statements by recognized authorities.

When you reach the end of your letter, after the proof, it is time to push for some kind of action. The simplest and most fundamental action-getter is to flatly ask for an order. Ask your prospect to buy and to buy now—today—without delay. If possible, give him reasons for avoiding delay. If there is a limited supply, tell him so. If you are offering a bargain price that will soon go up, tell him that. If the offer has a logical time limit on it, state it in a specific number of days.

Any legitimate means by which you can push your prospect into ordering *at once* will pay big dividends. People suffer greatly from inertia, and the prospect who was "almost" sold today will be twice as difficult to warm up tomorrow.

In writing your sales letter (or any other mail order copy for that matter), it is always best to use simple words, short phrases, and clear sentences that anyone can understand on the first reading. Don't be ambiguous. Don't use ornate terms or flowery phrases. Stay away from any attempt at phony sophistication or "fine writing" . . . including precious foreign words that only a college graduate who majored in Romance Languages could understand.

If you can get by with one vivid word, it isn't necessary to use two weaker ones. It is easy to say to yourself, "Well, a million people are going to read my letter, so what if a few of them don't get the message at first glance?" The best attitude to have (the *only* attitude to have) is to assume that you have only one prospect in the whole wide world, and only one chance to make the sale . . . and everything hinges on the way you phrase that one letter.

A further suggestion is that you strive for *plausibility* in your letter. It is easy to get so enthused about your product or offer that the copy to sell it comes out wholly unbelievable. Any copy that is destined to pull mail orders will be plausible, will cause your prospect to believe every word you say.

Another suggestion (indeed, an imperative) is that your copy express real sincerity. The absence or presence of sincerity in a letter can quickly be detected by your reader, and can either induce him to buy or cause him to reject the offer as sounding phony.

Sincerity can't be faked with any sustained degree of success. It stems from your own basic belief in yourself and your product. And if you have this belief and faith, the sincerity will shine through all your letters and ads.

Professional copywriters have been known to condescendingly describe the method of building a sales letter outlined here as mechanical or contrived. But if you have never written a sales letter, and you want to learn, this method will help you immensely. Remember, you merely line up your qualities and features, and turn them into selling phrases; then, like a chain of dominoes standing on end, you thump them over. Each one falls into the next, until you have made all your sales points in a smooth, effective manner.

Having used the qualities of your product as a blueprint for constructing your sales letter, you can similarly build in added impact by making a list of all the reasons why your prospect might *not* want to buy the products, and endeavoring to overcome these reasons within the body of the letter . . . before your reader has a chance to think of them himself, independently.

For instance, your prospect may think the price is too high, or he wants to buy but not just yet. In the first instance, you point out that the price may appear to be high, but when compared to products of a similar kind or of inferior make, it really is an exceptionally low price. Either that or you express the total price in such a way that it seems much lower than it actually is: "Only 10¢ per day pays for this Widgett," or "For less than you spend for cigarettes, you can own this handsome new Thingamajig."

If he wants to buy, but not right now, you must put some kind of penalty on waiting. This is easily done by offering him a cash discount for ordering immediately, or by offering a free premium if he places his order within a certain period of time.

Other objections that a prospect can make will occur to you if you make a deliberate effort to study and list the bad or negative qualities of your offer. Write them all down, and then figure out ways to overcome them. There are a dozen objections a prospect can make to buying your product, or reasons he can give for putting off the purchase, and it is your duty to anticipate as many of them as you can and *bring them into the letter* with corresponding reasons why he should not let these factors interfere with his immediate ownership and enjoyment of your product.

This has been an attempt to show you how to write a sales letter. All it can be is an attempt, because no one can really show you how to do it. The best that can be done is to describe a pattern or formula and make suggestions for following it, as we have done here. This chapter gives you one such formula. It is no better and no worse than a dozen others you will find in textbooks and courses on letter-writing. As stated in the beginnnig of the chapter, the best way to get a sales letter written is to have it done by a professional letter writer (one who writes *mail order* copy, not the typical ad agency type who suffers for days the creative throes of agonizingly composing a three-line piece for a client in the dry cleaning business).

The next best way is to sit down at the typewriter and do it yourself. In doing it yourself, it doesn't matter whether it comes out good or bad the first time. If you work at it, using this or some other pattern to go by, you're bound to come up with a pretty good letter . . . probably better than you think. You might even—as has happened repeatedly with people who have never before in their life written a sales letter— come up with the *perfect* letter for your product.

There is one tremendous advantage you have over a professional copywriter: Your product is one which you know personally and are enthusiastic about, and this enthusiasm will frequently make up for any technical deficiencies your letter might have.

Chapter 18

How to Get People
to Buy Your Product

The finger of science not only has probed around inside the atom and a thousand and one other natural phenomena, but in recent years it has poked deeper and deeper into the field of psychology to find out why people behave as they do.

The findings of one branch of this scientific investigation have proved immensely valuable to those engaged in the everyday business of selling, where the scientific data is put to work earning money.

The knowledge that psychologists have gained about people serves the advertising and sales industry extremely well, enabling sellers to create and stimulate demand for new products and services by making people *want* them. A working grasp of the basic psychological facts involved is indispensable in the conduct of a successful mail order business, since your success hinges entirely on how adept you are at making people want to buy what you have to sell.

Most of the things that psychologists have found out about people revolve around one central trait: They are, as individuals, *selfish*. (Not in the childish sense, but in the more general human sense.) This is not a criticism, but a demonstrably true aspect of the human animal. All this means is that your individual prospect is wrapped up in his own desires, ambitions, and aspirations. In short, he is interested in himself. And you must become interested in him, too, if you hope to sell him anything.

People also are susceptible to things which appeal to their emotions. They will get thoroughly agitated or enthused about something of no consequence whatsoever, provided it is dressed in the proper emotional form. Emotion can get sales action like nothing else can, and the most effective sales copy always contains one or more strong emotional appeals.

How you build emotion into sales copy is a difficult process to describe. Perhaps the most practical way is to search other ads and letters for headlines and copy that are particularly moving to your own emotions, then adapt the methods used to your own copy.

The various forms that individual "selfishness" takes have been classified, and it is important for you to be aware of these when you set out to compose sales letters and ad copy for your product. There are twenty-five basic reasons why people spend their money, and here they are:

To make money	To escape pain
To save money	To be praised
To save time	To be popular
To avoid effort	To attract the opposite sex
To achieve comfort	To conserve possessions
To achieve cleanliness	To realize pleasure
To enjoy good health	To gratify curiosity

To protect family	To avoid criticism
To be in style	To realize individuality
To own beautiful things	To take advantage of op-
To satisfy appetites	portunities
To emulate others	To avoid trouble
To be safe in making purchases	To protect their reputation

To sell anything to anybody anywhere, you *must* cater to one or more of these basic buying motives. This is as true in mail order as it is in personal selling . . . more so, because words-in-print are never as forceful as spoken words.

Fortunately, nearly every product you choose to handle will embody the satisfaction of one or more of the basic human wants, and your job will be to define those wants which a particular product satisfies, and then devise the selling phrases which connect a specific product feature with a specific buying motive.

Suppose you were selling a correspondence course in bookkeeping. Do you think anyone really wants to be a bookkeeper? Probably not; it's refined drudgery, at best. But to sell your course, you don't attempt to sell a prospect on the idea, per se, of being a bookkeeper. Instead you sell him the idea that he deserves a better-than-average income, a new car, a nice home, and the respect and envy of his less fortunate neighbors, and that a career in bookkeeping will help him get those things.

Take face cream. Do women really get a thrill out of smearing their faces with this unsightly, messy goop? Again, it is probable that they don't. (I've never personally asked one this particular question.) It is a more likely bet that the reason women smear their faces with this unsightly, messy goop is that in doing so they feel they are making themselves more attractive to their husbands, or other men, or both. To sell face cream, you don't sell face cream at all: You sell attractiveness and sex appeal.

Take Cadillacs. Do people really buy Cadillacs because they transport the body from X place to Y place? A Ford will do that. Do they spend $8,000 because a Cadillac rides easier than an Oldsmobile? Few people have the educated posteriors to tell the difference. No, people buy Cadillacs to satisfy one of the more pronounced human wants, that of *prestige*. That's the only reason, though few Caddy owners would admit it openly. Owning a Cadillac (or an Imperial, or a Rolls-Royce) sets them above and apart from those who have to be satisfied with Fords and Chevrolets . . . gives them the means to publicly display their status and thus acquire prestige.

Take certain highly touted novels. Do people read them because they enjoy them? In many cases, no. They read them because the ads scare them into believing that if they don't read them, they will be cultural and social outcasts. Nobody wants to be thought of as a social clod, and a person will go to almost any length—even to ruining his eyesight in the process of reading boring novels—to avoid becoming one. This illustrates our motives "to be in style" and "to avoid criticism."

If you could examine a dozen mail order offers that have failed, you probably would find that one of the causes of their failure (in some instances the *only* cause) is that the sales copy fails to present the product in terms of one or more of the basic human buying motives. Or, the copy will make a weak appeal to a less-important motive, completely ignoring several others of much greater importance to the prospective buyer.

A man recently went to his counselor with a line of desk nameplates, and a sales letter he had written to sell them with. The letter had been mailed to hundreds of prospects without producing a single sale. On reading the letter, the counselor immediately saw that the copy began and ended with matters of little or no importance whatever as sales appeal: the type of plastic used in the nameplates, the depth of the groove in the letters, and so on. Not a line appeared anywhere in the letter that went directly to one of the basic wants.

The counselor suggested that he be allowed to rewrite the letter, which he did. Instead of physical details, he gave the prospect personal, selfish reasons for wanting to buy the nameplate. Instead of telling him the nameplate was made of Tenite plastic, he pictured the nameplate as a handsome acquisition that would add dignity to his office, would remind visitors of his position and title, and would be a smart addition to his desk. The new sales letter was tried and worked extremely well.

You can spend your time most profitably in studying people and what makes them tick. This knowledge is important in mail order, and it can be a fascinating study, indeed, especially when you remember that the things you learn are going to mean hundreds and thousands of dollars to you.

This study is made in all sorts of ways: by rereading the list of basic buying motives previously given; by observing people in stores and shops and asking yourself, "What is the real reason that person is making that particular purchase?" by studying published ads and asking yourself which of the basic wants is being capitalized on; and by reading the sales letters you get in your daily mail to see how professional copywriters turn basic wants and motives into selling phrases.

Chapter 19

Testimonials: How to Get Them and How to Use Them

Nothing will help you more in selling products by mail than the consistent use of good testimonials. They are in a class with premiums and guarantees (about which we will have more to say later).

A testimonial will put teeth into your sales story for the simple reason that people may not believe what *you* have to say about your product in every case, but they will nearly always believe what a *satisfied user* has to say about it.

It is true that testimonials have been overworked in some areas of advertising and selling. People have come to be cynical and unimpressed by the use of testimonials from movie actors, famous golfers, and other public figures in praise of cigarettes and other products whose comparative merits are open to debate. But even these blatantly phony testimonials are partially effective.

Testimonials are especially valuable in selling a new product which has not been generally accepted by the public, or in selling an old product to a new market. In using testimonials, there are a few established rules to go by. One of these is that the testimonial must be *plausible,* or reasonable. It will defeat its purpose if it is so far-fetched—so exaggerated—as to sound trumped up or written by some kind of nut.

A firm selling a remedy for aches and pains steadily received testimonials from enthusiastic users of the product, but many of them were unusable in advertising because they were too implausible (even if, as in some cases, completely true). Some of the users would go so far as to say the remedy cured everything from heart trouble to cancer . . . and may have believed their own words.

You can't use testimonials that cannot be proved to be true. Thus, even if a user of a patent medicine writes and says that the product cured him of this or that, such a letter cannot lawfully be used in advertising, unless his statement can be proved scientifically by authorities in the field. The law takes the position that an average user is not qualified to pass on the real qualities of a medicine or panacea—only scientists can do this.

Whenever you use a testimonial, it has the legal status of your having made the same statements yourself. You can't print a testimonial in an ad, for example, and escape responsibility for its truthfulness by saying, "Well, that's what the user said in his letter."

Don't let the legal aspect of testimonials keep you from using them, however. Use testimonials in your sales material and in your ads, but be sure they are *plausible* and *true,* or at least provable.

Getting testimonials is not difficult if your product is a good one and fairly represented and sold. Some customers will, in fact, take it on themselves to write letters of testimony without your having to ask them

to do so. But if you are in a hurry to get some testimonials and don't want to wait for the unsolicited
ones to trickle in, you can do it by writing your customers and subtly asking them for a testimonial. There
are different ways to go about this, but one good way
is to compose a letter similar to the following and
send it out to users of your product:

> Dear Customer:
>
> By now, you have had a chance to use [your prod-
> uct] and have made up your mind about whether
> it's all we say it is. If you feel that it is, we'd appre-
> ciate hearing from you . . . and will send you a little
> surprise gift for your trouble. If it isn't, won't you let
> us know anyway?
>
> You see, a lot of folks want to use our product,
> but before buying, they'd like to hear what other
> users like yourself have to say about it. And we'd
> like to pass your opinion on to those future users,
> because we know your judgment and opinion will be
> respected.
>
> You can help us convince these future users by
> letting us know, on the enclosed form, what you think
> of our product. Just write it in your own words, as
> you would tell it to a neighbor or friend. Our future
> customers will appreciate it just as much as we do.

Along with this letter you send a form (which
can be mimeographed) that provides space for the
customer to write in his testimonial. At the top of this
form you can put a statement like this: "I am ....,
am not ...., more than happy with your [name of
product] for the following reasons:"

Near the bottom of the form you provide a "release," worded in a manner similar to this: "This gives you my permission to use the above statements in your advertising and sales literature. Date ....
Signed .... "

On receipt of the signed testimonial and release, you then send your customer an inexpensive gift, such as a ball-point pen, to show your gratitude and to establish consideration for the release.

In those instances where a testimonial comes in unsolicited, you should write the customer and obtain his permission to use his letter, asking him to sign a release form like that given above. Releases are necessary for photographs as well as written statements, and don't fail to get them in all cases before using testimonials in your ads and printed material.

Some of your customers will be glad to have you use their statements, but will prefer that their full names be withheld. So it is a good idea to provide spaces on your release form for the customer to indicate whether his full name or just his initials may be used.

In all cases, keep your original testimonial letters on file—preferably in a fireproof cabinet or safe. At some point along the way you may be asked by the postal authorities to produce the originals, and it can be embarrassing not to be able to do so.

Chapter 20

Guarantees: a Powerful Aid to Mail Selling

A good rule in mail order is this: *Never handle anything you can't guarantee.*

Stated backwards, it still makes sense: *Guarantee everything that you sell.*

A guarantee is one of the simplest, most powerful aids to mail selling you can employ. Yet the number of would-be mail order operators who stubbornly refuse to, or half-heartedly use a guarantee is appalling.

Guarantees should be used at all times, but they are especially important to the success of a new product and/or a new venture. When you arrive on the mail order scene with new products, you will be unknown, with no established record of fair dealing to convey your reliability and integrity. In this situation a strong, comprehensive guarantee on all your products can help pave the way to faster success.

Guarantees are of many types, but the most commonly used one is the basic "Satisfaction guaranteed or your money back." This guarantee is said to have originated in the nineteenth century with a man named Sears . . . who subsequently developed one of the world's largest enterprises, Sears, Roebuck and Co. It is also said, with a great deal of justification, that this simple guarantee was more responsible for the firm's huge success than any other single factor. It isn't hard to see why. For in those days a guarantee was unheard of. The rule of selling was "Let the buyer beware." Then along came a man who had the unprecedented courage to stand behind his products with the world's first blanket money-back guarantee.

The use of a guarantee never costs the operator a cent if he is selling a worthwhile product. Most people are honest in money matters and ask only that you send them what you say you will in your ads and sales literature. If you deceive them, they naturally have a right to—and usually will—squawk to the postal authorities. Of course, there are a certain number of professional gripers in the world who would not be happy with anything you sent them, but they are in the minority, and their existence is one of the occupational nuisances of the mail order business (or any other business, for that matter). You will inevitably run into some of these people as you go along, but if you know your product is good and are willing to stand behind your guarantee, you have nothing to fear.

While guarantees don't cost anything, except a little extra paperwork and postage every now and then, they can be highly instrumental in stimulating sales. Many more people will buy a guaranteed product than will buy one that isn't. One mail order operator didn't quite believe this . . . although he believed in his product. Finally his counselor prevailed upon him to put an iron-clad guarantee on his product, and sales went up nearly fifty percent. True, his refunds went up about five percent, but that represented a small price to pay for a very healthy increase in business.

Another good rule in mail selling is this: *Don't make any guarantee that you are not fully prepared to back up.* Nothing will get a customer so excited as welching on a guarantee. To renege on one is to invite a visit by the postal inspectors, and it won't be a social call. Bear in mind that when you have to make a refund, said refund doesn't cost you the selling price of the product; it costs you only the shipping and postage involved, in most cases. If the product is returned undamaged, it can be resold.

Unusual guarantees are a way of putting originality into an otherwise staple or run-of-the-mill product. One firm has sold millions of dollars worth of a specialty product by guaranteeing that the user of the product will realize $10 from the use of the item for each dollar the product costs him. This is an irresistible guarantee, particularly when it is made clear that it is genuine and will be backed up.

Nowadays, of course, the mass merchandisers have stumbled onto this truth about guarantees that mail order people have known for years. Many kinds of products are being guaranteed "for life," automobiles are being guaranteed "for five years," and so on.

A mail order guarantee should have a time limit of some kind on it, beyond which the customer cannot ask for a refund. This is to prevent him from sending the product back two or three years later, when he happens to need a few dollars, under the guise of being dissatisfied with it. Time limits are variable, depending on the product. Books, as a rule, are allowed five to thirty days to be returned. Mechanical devices usually must be returned within ninety days. Highly durable goods might be returnable for as long as six months.

Don't fail to use guarantees in your business—individual product guarantees as well as a blanket company guarantee that covers everything you sell. Unusual and out-of-the-ordinary guarantees are good, too, and should be tried any time the product or situation warrants.

Chapter 21

Premiums: How to Make Money by Giving Things Away Free

Webster defines a premium as "an extra reward or recompense."

Salesmen, including mail sellers, call premiums the greatest device to stimulate sales ever conceived. And they're right.

Properly selected and used, a premium can put profit into an otherwise unprofitable offer. Or it can put extra profit into an already profitable one. It can sell things by mail that otherwise couldn't be sold at all through mail order channels.

No matter what you are now selling or plan to sell by mail, you can probably enhance its earning potentialities by judiciously choosing a premium to go along with it.

There came in the mail the other day a mailing piece from an outfit selling a very commonplace item —mimeograph paper. If you were to poll a dozen well-known mail order operators, they would no doubt be unanimous in stating that such a staple product, available everywhere at low cost, could not profitably be sold by mail. But this particular firm is doing it successfully, and they are doing it on the strength of a powerful premium offer.

The major book clubs could not thrive as they do except by going all-out for premium offers. A New York office supply firm could not have built a list of over a million customers throughout the United States without the continued use of premiums. A lot of successful newcomers to mail order would not be successful without an understanding and skillful use of premiums.

Many moribund merchandisers, of course, fail to see the handwriting on the wall and stubbornly refuse to use premiums. "I'd rather go broke than give something away free" is their attitude. And that occasionally is what happens.

You are not, as you can see, actually giving something away free. You are making use of a premium to force the sale of another item, in which there is enough profit to make the total transaction a satisfying one to everybody concerned.

There is a lure to a free premium that is hard to resist, provided of course that it really is *free* (and it must be to conform to the law). Witness the fantastic success of the so-called trading stamps used by food stores, drug stores, and many others. Trading stamps have little value in themselves, often representing one percent or less in actual savings to the consumer. But millions of shoppers slavishly buy merchandise at those stores that give stamps, in preference to those that don't. As a matter of fact, a lot of shoppers will trade at a store that gives trading stamps (realizing a net saving of one or two percent), rather than go to another store that doesn't give stamps but offers im-

mediate cash savings of five to ten percent. It's foolish
and unreasonable, but true nevertheless.

The principle of the free premium is the same
whether used in the grocery business or the mail order
business, and can be just as effective for one as for
the other.

In using premiums to stimulate the sale of *your*
product, you must remember that a premium has to
be free . . . with no strings attached. This doesn't
mean that you can hike the price of your product up
enough to cover the cost of the premium; not in very
many cases, anyway. The premium must be something
over and above the product, and its cost must usually
be absorbed out of your normal product profit margin.

You may object that such a practice will increase
your selling costs. True. But it is also true that your
gross sales will increase (often tremendously), resulting perhaps in more cost in each product but definitely
in more total sales and net profit on over-all operations.
Suppose, for example, that you can normally sell fifty
orders of a given product at an average price of $2,
without the use of premiums. Suppose further that
you can throw in a premium that costs you twenty-
five cents and drive your gross sales up to a hundred
orders at an average of $2. Would it be worth doing?

There is a popular delusion among some businessmen, beginners and old pros alike, that it is better to
take a *large* profit on a *few* sales than a lower profit
on a much bigger volume of sales. This delusion has
nipped many promising businesses in the bud. The
real smart cookies in business these days don't try to
make all their money on one customer. They realize

it's better to make a ten percent net profit of $100,000 worth of business than it is to make forty percent on $5,000 worth.

A premium must not only be free, but it must *have value in itself.* It must be something that your typical prospect would like to possess. Something that is entertaining, instructive, informative, utilitarian, or a combination of those.

A premium can be related or unrelated to the product you're selling, but in no case should it satisfy the desire for the main offer. That is, your premium should not parallel the use or appeal of your main offer to the degree that if your customer owns the premium, he has less reason to own the main product. On the contrary, a good premium is one that whets the appetite for the main offer.

One of the easiest ways for a mail order firm to develop a premium program is to start issuing free certificates with the purchase of items, each certificate entitling the buyer to a discount on future purchases. This not only stimulates initial sales but results in additional business. It is possibly the widest used of all premium plans in mail order and is adaptable to any product or service. Suppose you are selling an instruction manual on a certain subject. To the purchaser of that manual you send along a printed certificate giving him a specific discount when he buys some of the other books in your line. In fact, this certificate can be worth the same amount as he paid for the first manual thus making his first purchase free but causing him to come back for several books or manuals on related subjects.

The law is pretty strict in regard to the use of premiums. Formerly, you could not advertise a premium unless you were willing to send it without requiring the purchase of something. Thus, if you advertised an item as being free, you could not ask that something else be purchased at the same time to get the free item. You had to send the premium to anyone who wrote in for it, whether they bought or not.

However, the law has been relaxed to the extent that you can now require the purchase of an item in order to entitle the customer to the free premium, provided the cost of the product has not been altered to cover the cost of the premium. You cannot legitimately raise the selling price of your product to also cover the cost of the thing you give away. This, according to the law, is deception.

To be on the safe side, it is a good idea, when using premiums, to state clearly in your ads and letters that the customer will get the free gift or premium when he orders the main proposition, but the premium is his to keep even though he should choose to send the product back for a refund. This works very well, not only in stimulating sales but in promoting confidence in your firm.

In all forms of mail order the purpose of a premium is not only to get your prospect to order but to order *quickly*. So it is a good idea, when offering a premium, to put a time limit on it. That is, an order must be received within a certain period of time, or before such-and-such a date, in order to entitle the customer to the free gift.

For a premium to be effective, it frequently isn't enough that it be something of value. You may have to give the premium itself a good sales pitch in order to create a desire for it. Even though it is valuable, and free, you must work hard at making your prospect want it. In fact, many direct-mail offers devote more sales effort to generating a desire for the free premium than they do to trying to sell the product itself . . . on the sound theory that if you can make the premium sound good enough, the prospect will buy the main offer almost sight unseen in order to get the premium.

Use premiums whenever and wherever you can. But always be sure they are free, have value, and are worth acquiring.

Chapter 22

How to Build a Mailing List

If you plan to sell by direct mail, it is not enough to have a superb product and a wonderful sales letter. You must, in addition, have the names and addresses of the people who are logical prospects for your product. And you must have enough of these names that you can continue to send out your mailings without running out of prospects.

Fortunately, getting an adequate supply of names is no longer a problem for most firms, provided it is definitely known what type of prospect is needed. Before you set out in search of a thousand or a million prospects' names, you have to first decide the kind of prospect you want, and this—obviously—is determined by what you are selling.

Should you be selling a book on how to make money, then your best prospects would be people who have bought money-making books from other firms. Should you decide to sell a line of sporting goods, you could get the names of known mail order sporting goods buyers.

The business of supplying name-and-address lists has kept pace with the growth of the mail order business and is in itself a large segment of the industry.

As you know, or will learn, there are several large firms (for the most part located in New York) whose business it is to supply you with names and addresses of many different classes of mail order prospects, in virtually any quantity. The names of these mailing-list houses can easily be gotten by writing to other mail order firms or by subscribing to the mail trade journals, such as *The Reporter of Direct Mail Advertising,* where you will see their various ads. (For addresses of mail trade and other advertising publications, see your librarian or a copy of *Standard Rate & Data Service for Business Publications.*)

Whether you plan to purchase name lists in the immediate future or not, it will pay you to write one or more of the prominent list houses and request their catalog. It won't cost you anything, but it will give you an understanding of the list business and how it can serve your own future needs.

There are additional sources of names which you can use. One of the best is other mail order firms. Many mail order operators will be more than willing to rent you lists of their customers and inquirers, provided you are not in direct competition with them as far as your product is concerned.

Telephone directories have some value as mailing-list sources, particularly if you are selling to businesses and professional people. Should you need a list of department stores, for example, you could readily compile one from the yellow pages of the telephone books. Most telephone companies—including out-of-town ones —will be more than glad to sell you copies of their current directories. They aren't expensive, ranging in price from twenty-five cents for very small towns to $2 or so for the large cities.

The accuracy of any given mailing list will not usually be greater than ninety-five percent, although most legitimate list sources make intensive efforts to keep their lists "clean," removing inactive names and correcting addresses. In planning your mailing, make allowance in your costs for the approximately five percent of your letters that will be undeliverable.

Other sources of mailing lists are city directories, trade and association directories, membership and subscription lists.

Names cost money, of course. Whether you compile them yourself or buy them from a mailing-list house, they will cost you anywhere from $10 to $25 per thousand. In setting up your schedule of selling costs, be sure to allow for the cost of the names. You will also have to pay for getting the names typed on your envelopes, unless the list source includes this service. (In dealing with a list house, you normally have an option as to whether you want the names on gummed labels, file cards, or directly addressed on your envelopes.)

Most reliable list houses offer a free consultation service, which is quite valuable if you are not sure what type of prospects you should mail to. If you are in doubt, write your list house or source explaining what you have to sell and including specimens of your sales literature. They will, in most cases, be able to suggest the best lists for you to use.

If you plan to sell exclusively from space ads in magazines or newspapers, then you won't have a list problem. You will, after a while, be able to compile a list of your own customers and inquirers, which you can then turn around and rent or sell to other mail order firms. This provides you with an additional source of revenue and profit. For this reason, it will pay you to set your names up on an addressing machine in alphabetical, geographical order, as they are received.

Chapter 23

How to Key Your Ads

Before describing some of the innumerable ways to key your ads, perhaps we should first discuss the why of keying ads. If you have never run any display or classified ads in newspapers and magazines, the reason for keying, or coding, may be somewhat obscure to you.

Let's approach it this way. Suppose you were selling a certain product by mail, and you decided to put the same ad in two different magazines at the same time. Suppose also that you had had no prior experience with either of these two magazines, but you had heard that they both were good "pullers." If you ran the same ad in both magazines simultaneously, once the orders started coming in, how would you know which magazine pulled which order?

You wouldn't, unless the ads were keyed. The reason you want to know which magazine pulled which orders is so you can get some clear idea of which is the best magazine to use in the future. If the two magazines containing your ad pulled a hundred orders in the aggregate, and the ads were not keyed, you would have no way of knowing how many orders to attribute to each magazine.

Conceivably, out of the hundred orders, one magazine might have pulled ninety orders and the other magazine only ten orders. (There can be that much difference between magazines having ostensibly the same circulation and type of readership.) Naturally, if this occurred, you would not want to spend any more money on the magazine that pulled only ten orders.

The foregoing is a simplified illustration, but the lesson is clear. The process of keying ads can be valuable not only in telling which publications pull the best, but in other ways as well. Some companies, for instance, will run not just one but two or three ads in the same magazine at the same time, on the same product, to determine the effect of position. And when you are running the same ad month after month, keying it will eventually tell you what the seasonal characteristics of the magazine are; i.e., which months produce the most orders per dollar spent.

The mechanics of keying an ad are as varied as you want them to be. One way is to change your mailing address slightly from one ad to another, and one publication to another. Mail order buyers always address their orders exactly as your address appears in the ad, and there is little danger of their omitting the key when it is part of your address. If the ad shows your address to be "601 E. 4th St.," you can key it the next time by changing it to read "601 East Fourth St.," and the next by making it read "601 East 4th Street." Or you can throw in a letter of the alphabet (provided it won't confuse your postman) like this: "601-A E. Fourth St."

Another way to key ads is to include a department number. For one ad you can use "Dept. A," for another, "Dept. B." Some firms expedite matters by using the magazine's initials in the department key: An ad in *Better Homes & Gardens* would thus be keyed "Dept. BHG." The department number, of course, appears in addition to your regular address. The only disadvantage of using a department-number key is that it sounds a bit ostentatious when the advertiser obviously is a very small company. It also takes up extra space, which can be an important factor in small ads.

If you use a post office box, you can easily key the box number. For instance, if your box number is 211, you can make it read "P. O. Box 211-A" in one ad, "P. O. Box 211-B" in the next, and "P. O. Box 211-C" in the third.

Your firm name offers all sorts of keying opportunities. If you do business as John B. Doe, you can key one ad by using the name "J. B. Doe" and another by using "John Bertram Doe."

If your ads include a coupon, you can key them in any of the ways described, or be content with the built-in key which coupons automatically contain. That is, the reverse side of the coupon will tell you which issue of a magazine it appeared in, since ads are shifted around from one spot to another from one issue to the next, and the back side of your coupon will have portions of ads and editorial matter from that particular issue.

Direct mail is also easily keyed. It can be done by putting a symbol or letter of the alphabet on the return envelope or order form. Or you can simply change the color of order forms and envelopes from one mailing to the next.

In regard to keying, it is a good idea to work up a chart showing all the keys you are using and post this in your office or shipping room so it can be referred to as the orders come in.

Also, it is good practice to show on your order forms and customer file cards just where each order originated, and its date of receipt. Later on this can be of value in making long-range appraisals of mailings and media.

Chapter 24

Printers and Printing: What You Should Know About Each

Perhaps nothing is so important in mail order as *good printing*. You can compromise and hedge on the other tools of your business, but you dare not do so on your printing.

That's because the only contact you have with your customer is through printing. If your printing is superior, he is more inclined to believe that you and your product are superior. If your printing is shoddy, he may feel the opposite.

As every mail order counselor and operator knows, even a bad piece of copy will usually produce some orders if it is handsomely printed on quality paper. But the best copy in the world will fall flat if it is poorly printed on cheap-quality stock.

In setting up your mail venture, there are a few printing essentials you must have at once to get off to a good start. These will require a modest outlay of capital, but as you'll discover later on, they are more than worth it.

For one thing, you'll need a quantity of letterheads. Although you may plan to sell directly from magazine ads, involving no sales letters, catalogs, or reply envelopes, you will still need letterheads on which to correspond with sources of supply, answer complaints, and answer special requests.

You don't have to buy a great quantity of letter-heads in the beginning, but those you buy should be of good quality, well printed on a good grade of bond paper. They don't have to be flashily done up in two or three colors; you can get by with a simple black-and-white job if the type styles and layout are carefully selected and arranged. The minimum quantity of letterheads you can economically buy is five hundred to a thousand. (The same is true of nearly any other kind of printing.) This quantity of letterheads, in one color on twenty-pound white bond paper, will cost you anywhere from $10 to $20, depending on the printer. A few mail order printers offer to do the job for less, but as a rule, the saving you make is not worthwhile, considering the delays and postage involved.

Letterheads call for matching envelopes, and you will need a similar quantity of these, costing anywhere from $9 to $18, again depending on the printer. Shipping labels also will be required, but you can usually get by at the start by purchasing stock labels at the office-supply store. Later on, when your volume of business justifies it, you can have your own labels printed at a cost of about $7.50 per thousand.

Reply envelopes are essential to a successful mail operation, and you should include them in your printing outlay. These will cost you from $7 to $11, whether you use the unstamped or business-reply type.

Some beginners attempt to get by with a rubber stamp to save the cost of printing letterheads and envelopes. A rubber stamp has its value in the mail order business (for endorsing checks, etc.) but should never be used in the place of good printing. Its use immediately marks the user as an amateur.

The subject of printing brings up the subject of printers. Whether you like it or not—and it can get to be a chore—you have to deal with printers. Many of them are downright incompetent; a number of them know their trade but for some reason or other don't always pass their skill along to their customer in the form of good printing; and of course, a lot of them are reputable businessmen who will try hard to give you a fair price on a decent printing job.

The difference in quality of work among different printers is often vast indeed. The same is true of their prices. In time you will be able to locate and use a printer who combines the happy medium of quality, price, and service, but if you make a few mistakes in judgment in the beginning, you won't be unusual.

In general, when dealing with printers, always get a written estimate or quotation on a printing job before you place the order. Make sure that such quotation specifies the type of paper that is going to be used, and obtain samples of the paper when you get the quotation.

Once you have a quotation from one printer, take your job specifications to another printer and get another estimate or quotation. (*Don't* show the second printer the quotation you got from the first.) After enough estimates have been acquired in this manner, you can then make up your own mind as to which printer is the one to use.

It is also a good idea to make the printer show you samples of work he has done for others, of a kind similar to yours. This is particularly important when you are buying a job that involves photographs (or halftones, as they are called), a job using more than one color of ink, or a job where there is to be a lot of solid-ink coverage. Printers differ widely on these points, owing to the differences in presses used.

Chapter 25

Mail Order Questions and Answers

What Fields of Business Present the Best Mail Order Opportunities Today?

This is difficult to answer. However, there appears to be room for, and a need for, new mail order businesses in the office-supply field, in the business-information field, in the printing-specialties field, in credit-and-collection aids and ideas, and in syndicated advertising pieces of all kinds. There is a continuing need for good information in the business-plans and self-help book field. And, of course, there is always opportunity in the consumer-goods field, selling everything from fishing lures for sportsmen to automobile specialties for car owners to household items for homeowners.

Is It Necessary To Have a Completely Original Idea or Product To Succeed in Mail Order?

Definitely not. Many so-called original mail order ideas are merely adaptations or switches on old ideas. Most successful mail order ideas consist of 1) finding a fresh way of selling an old product; 2) introducing a standard product into a brand-new market by discovering new uses for it; 3) reviving a product which has faded from public view, but which has a strong appeal to a new generation of buyers; 4) modifying an obsolete product to fit a modern market.

How Many Mail Order Businesses Are There in The United States?

Figures vary, but best estimates set the number at or near ten thousand.

What Is the Future for a Small Mail Order Business?

Practically unlimited for a well-managed one offering good products or services at fair prices. The country is growing at an astounding rate, and this fact means opportunity for growth and expansion at a similar rate.

What Is the Average Yearly Profit of the Ten Thousand Mail Order Businesses Now Operating?

Only the Department of Internal Revenue can tell you that. The average is probably somewhere around $10,000. But this can be misleading, because many small operations make little or nothing, while others show annual net profits of $50,000 or more. The amount depends almost entirely on the skill and abilties of the individual operator.

*Why Are So Many People Interested in Mail Order
. . . and Why Do So Few Actually Wind Up with
Their Own Businesses?*

Because there are more wishful thinkers than there are doers. It is one thing to be interested in making money, but quite another to do something about it. Why are there so many employ*ees*, and so few employ*ers*? Why are some folks content to spend their lives running elevators and punching time clocks? It is not a lack of opportunity that prevents these people from having businesses of their own, but rather a lack of initiative, desire, ability, or sufficient motivation.

How Many People Actually Buy by Mail?

There are no published figures on this. But literally millions. For instance, in one representative year nearly six million people bought seeds and plants by mail, over a hundred thousand bought kitchen utensils from one firm, nearly half a million bought postage stamps for collections, nearly a quarter million bought weight-reducing tablets, nearly twenty thousand ordered bronzed baby shoes, over a hundred thousand ordered a home repair book, seventy-five thousand inquired about a course in electroplating, over a hundred thousand bought a welding machine, and so on, ad infinitum. These are just a few random examples to give you an idea of the range and scope of mail order. There are thousands more, but these are sufficient to establish the fact that mail order is truly big business.

What Kind of Product Is a Beginner Most Likely To Be Successful With?

Those products he knows best and likes to handle most. A beginner should not force himself to handle a product he doesn't like, or isn't personally familiar with, even though he thinks it will sell.

How Can a Trade or Profession Be Put to Use in Mail Order?

If you are lucky enough to be trained in some trade or profession, your best opportunity for success and satisfaction in mail order will be in finding or creating products relating to your specialized training. An electronics technician would do best handling a line of electronics specialties; an accountant would be happier selling record forms or systems; a mechanic would find satisfaction selling auto parts or specialties; a pharmacist would find his mail order opportunity in packaging chemical compounds or formulas.

How Many Products Should a Beginner Start With?

Except in unsual cases, not more than one or two. But he should be prepared to add to these by staying on the lookout for potentially good sellers.

What Is the Federal Government's Attitude Toward Mail Order?

The Federal Government favors and encourages the development of legitimate mail enterprises. It is good for the economy, good for small business, and contrary to popular opinion, good for the efficient operation of the Post Office Department.

Is It a Good Idea To Borrow Money To Finance a Mail Business?

No. Mail order has a high element of chance in it, and there's no such thing as a *sure* thing . . . neither in mail order nor in any other phase of business. Borrowed money might be used to purchase equipment and other items that have lasting value, but don't use it to finance an ad or direct-mail campaign until long after such campaigns have already been proved successful.

If a Person Owns a Small Retail Store, Should He Sell it To Go into Mail Order?

Definitely not, unless the store is operating at a loss, in which case he will want to sell it, anyway. A retail store can be instrumental in the success of a mail order enterprise, because it means you already have established wholesale sources, space to work in, and possibly a good line of credit. Many operators have found the combination of retailing and mail order to be an ideal way to build a volume of business. Owning a store can help offset the dull mail order seasons by providing you with a flow of local business, and vice versa. Mail selling techniques can often be adapted at the local level to increase the amount of retail business a store produces.

Is a Rural Resident Under a Handicap in Mail Order Work?

Living on a farm or in a small village is no handicap in mail order, with the possible exception of making it difficult to get your mail rapidly. A rural address is no handicap at all as a business address.

How Much Better Is a New York or Chicago Address Than a Small-Town Address?

Practically none, except for some specialized products, such as business publications and technical services. The general trend is away from the city, except for certain occupational groups. A small-town address is just as good as a big-city address. The important thing is not the address but the person behind the address. Some of the nation's most successful mail businesses are located in small towns.

Is It True That Anything Can Be Sold by Mail?

No . . . not *as is*. But nearly anything can be sold by mail provided it is given the right twist in price, guarantee, premium, or terms of sale. Relatively few staple products can be sold by mail without first giving them some unusual twist.

What Is the Surest "Sure Thing" in Mail Order?

The class of goods that comes nearest to being a "sure thing" in mail order is that which embraces the self-help and instruction field; i.e., books, manuals, and correspondence courses. Although this class of goods doesn't always represent the biggest profit potential, it usually does offer the greatest safety.

Is There a Magic Formula or a "Big Secret" to Mail Order?

Certainly not. Those who say there is are merely capitalizing on the gullibility of naïve people. The biggest mail successes often will be the first to debunk the myth of "big secrets." Some of them will even be glad to take you through their plants, let you study their literature and talk with their personnel . . . learn everything about their business, in fact. They are secure in doing this because they realize that the only secret in mail order is hard work, determination, sound management, and imagination . . . more or less in that order. Any of the several good books on the subject of mail order will tell you all the "secrets" there are. The rest is up to you.

Is It True That a Single Small Ad Often Will Pull a Fortune?

Most of the stories you read or hear about somebody getting rich from one ad are purely fictitious. There have been—and will continue to be—very rare instances in which an advertiser pulls a large amount of business from one insertion of one ad. One such case reports a man spending $100 for a newspaper ad and receiving nearly $40,000 worth of orders. Another is said to have pulled close to half-a-million dollars worth of business from one full-page ad in a national magazine. But these are exceptions, not the rule. It takes even a good ad several insertions to pull its maximum number of orders, and the ad must be repeated steadily if it is to continue to pull.

Is There Any Scientific Way To Take the Gamble out of Mail Order?

No. The success of a mail venture—like show biz–– is dependent solely on the reactions of the public to your offer, and the public does not often lend itself to the precise manipulations of a slide rule, except in psychological terms. Dealing with the public is an art, not a science. Science does play its part in mail order, however, particularly the science of statistics, which is used to measure and check the effectiveness of direct-mail or ad pull. But science won't *get* the orders for you; it can only tell you whether you got them at a profit and whether you should repeat or extend a given promotional effort.

Is It True That a Mail Order Business Can Be Expanded to Great Size Just by Running More Ads in More Magazines?

Yes, provided your ad has been proved not just once but several times to be a steady puller, and provided further that you can find enough good magazines to run it in. For example, one firm ran a one-inch ad in one magazine all year long, pulling a total of

$5,000 worth of business for an ad cost of about $2,000. A second magazine of the same general type was added, and it too pulled an aggregate of $5,000 in orders for approximately the same ad cost. Other magazines were gradually tested and added until the company was grossing over $50,000 a year. This feature of building a business simply by increasing the number of ads run is one of the most attractive aspects of mail order. In following such a plan, you must be careful, making sure at each step of the way that the magazines pull a profitable number of orders for each dollar spent. This is a matter of testing.

Should a Beginner Employ an Advertising Agency?

The advice and counsel of an experienced ad agency can be extremely valuable to a beginner. However, there are only a handful of legitimate ad agencies who cater to the mail order trade (or have any thorough-going mail order experience themselves), and they won't usually handle a newcomer unless he is prepared to spend anywhere from $50 up for consultation service and $200 or so per month for ad space. Normally, a legitimate agency's services do not cost you anything, except for specific items of copy and artwork they are required to do for you. Its compensation is derived from the cost of the advertising space you use, based on fifteen percent of the amount you spend. This is paid to the agency by the publisher, not by you. Only recognized agencies are allowed this commission, and the space costs you, the advertiser, the same amount whether you place your ad through an agency or direct. Since the amount an agency earns on a small ad is fairly low, you can see that it cannot afford to give you very much time and attention for so little compensation. Once your account has grown to the point at which you are spending $1,000 or more per month, however, it will not be difficult to get an agency interested in your account.

Should a Beginner Work at Home or Rent an Office?

Work at home, by all means, unless you already occupy an office or store and can handle your mail business there. One of the nice things about mail order is that it doesn't make much difference where you set up shop . . . in the corner of a bedroom, in the garage, or in the attic. You don't meet your customers face-to-face, so you don't have to put on any front. If you have the space, work at home until you see whether your project is going over or not. Doing this will help conserve your capital.

How Much Equipment Should a New Operation Have To Start With?

The less money you tie up in equipment at the start, the better off you'll be. However, there are certain indispensable items that you must have to conduct your business in a businesslike way. You'll need a small postal scale, for one thing, to weigh your outgoing packages and letters. You'll need a typewriter, though this can be rented in the beginning. You'll need a small 3″ x 5″ card file, with cards on which to keep your customer records. You'll need shelves and racks to hold your stock and mailing materials, but these can be fashioned out of spare lumber or crates. Your correspondence will call for a place to file carbon copies of letters, as well as original order letters and inquiries. These files can be orange-crates or heavy corrugated boxes partitioned to accommodate the letters and orders. You'll also need a small desk, a typing table, and possibly a large table to be used for packing and shipping purposes. In addition, you may need a gummed-tape dispenser (plus several rolls of tape), and a roll of brown wrapping paper. Incidentals include a stamp dispenser, letter opener, rubber stamp for endorsing checks and money orders, dating stamp, paper clips, and rubber bands.

Should a Beginner Attempt To Issue a Catalog?

A catalog is probably the best all-around mail selling tool. The problem it presents to the beginner, however, is the selection of a wide range of items to go into it (and arranging for a multitude of supply sources), as well as the high initial cost of preparing and printing the catalog. The average beginner would be wise to try one or more single products in the beginning, and as good sellers are found, keep adding to them until a *line* of products is being handled. When you have such a line, then it becomes feasible to put all of your products into catalog form and promote the catalog through ads and direct mail.

How Elaborate Should a Catalog Be?

A catalog can be any size and length, from a brief four-page folder listing just a few products to the thousand-page job issued by such giants as Montgomery Ward. A catalog can be printed in black and white on ordinary paper and still be effective, but full color illustrations on glossy stock obviously will be even more so. Catalogs as a whole do a good selling job because they are not thrown away as other types of literature are. Compiling a catalog requires special art-and-copy know-how (not to mention special merchandising know-how), and it is wise to enlist the aid of experienced professionals when undertaking a project of this kind.

What About the Companies Who Offer To Supply Ready-Made Catalogs with Individual Imprints?

There are a number of companies around, in the gift and housewares field, which will provide you with preprinted mail order catalogs illustrating several dozen to several hundred products. These catalogs have no company name on them. You place your order for a quantity of them (usually a thousand or more) and *your* name is imprinted in the appropriate space. The cost of these catalogs varies, but usually is on the order of $100 per thousand. You are supposed to buy the catalogs, mail them out to your prospects, and then relay the orders received to the wholesale suppliers, whose names are on a list sent with the catalogs. You receive a commission on each sale, ranging from twenty-five to fifty percent. This allegedly puts you in the mail order business, with no inventory to carry or any expenditure other than the cost of the catalogs, mailing list, and postage. The trouble with deals of this kind is that usually the catalogs are poorly produced or are filled with a lot of merchandising lemons that won't sell enough to cover your costs. A number of the companies operating the syndicated-catalog idea are not interested in selling merchandise at all, but make their money selling high-priced printing. They prepare the catalogs in huge quantities at low cost, then dole them out to a multitude of small mailers a thousand or more at a time, at a large profit to themselves. The dead giveaway on most catalog schemes of this kind is the question, "If this catalog pulls as well as they say it does, why are they letting *me* in on it? Why don't they mail all the catalogs themselves and keep all the profit?" Aside from that, the principal disadvantage of preprinted catalogs is that the same customers receive several copies of the same catalog, but all bearing different company names and addresses, and this makes the whole operation ludicrous. There are a couple of exceptions to the foregoing, of course, where the firm preparing the catalogs in the first place makes an honest effort to produce a catalog that will actually pull a profitable number of orders. Such catalogs are prepared by mail order firms who have already been successful in consumer selling, and compile their catalogs around their proven sellers. Such catalogs can be used at a profit if you already have a list of *customers* who have bought something from you through magazine ads or direct mail. It is not advisable to send a quantity of these catalogs out to "cold" mailing lists; doing so will rarely ever produce a profit.

What Is the Mortality Rate Among New Mail Order Companies?

No exact data is available on this, but it is said that about fifty percent of all new mail ventures fail within the first year, and only about twenty-five percent manage to survive the first two or three years.

What Are the Major Causes of Failure?

Some fail through lack of capital or proper management. But most fail through lack of mail order know-how, lack of willingness to take the right chance at the right time, lack of attention to the important details of the business, lack of a good product "sense," and similar reasons.

Mail Order Questions and Answers

199
Is It True That People Throw Letters Away Without Reading Them?

Yes, but they never throw one away without first knowing what it's about. Some otherwise astute merchandisers won't use direct mail, in the erroneous belief that their letters will be thrown in the wastebasket unopened. If this were true, half the direct-mail outfits in the country would be out of business. The fact of the matter is that any sales letter will get enough attention to show the prospect what it is about. No one, not even the biggest business executive, is going to throw a letter away without first determining whether it contains something new and useful to him. It is this fact that proves the importance of a good "opener" in a sales letter. The open (as well as the "teaser" on the outside of the envelope) usually decides the fate of the mailing piece . . . whether it goes sailing into "File 13" or goes back on the desk for a more careful reading.

How Do You Go About Finding New Products?

Staying on the alert for new products to sell by mail is one of the most important functions of a successful mail order operator. There is no specific way to go about this. In general, it is accomplished by keeping your eyes and ears open and lining up good current information sources. You can watch your state and local newspapers for reports of new items produced in your neighborhood or region. You can scan the merchandise sections of national papers such as the *New York Times* and the *Journal of Commerce*. It helps to buy samples or subscriptions to trade journals in the fields that interest you. Watch the mail trade magazines. Set up an idea file, and whenever you see a likely-looking item file it away for future consideration. When you think of an original idea that has possibilities, write it down in outline form and put it in your file. Observe products being sold by your competitors and others in mail order. Attend the periodic trade shows that are held in major distribution areas of the United States.

Can Postcards Be Used To Sell by Direct Mail?

Only in a very limited way. There is no record of a major mail order success being built around the government postcard as its prime advertising format. (Adaptations and elaborations of the postcard—such as large self-mailers—are, of course, a staple of the direct-mail business.) The postcard does have its use, however, especially for acknowledging inquiries and orders, because it is inexpensive and travels via first-class mail.

What Kind of Products Are Not Suited to Mail Selling?

Elsewhere in this book we have given a list of the positive qualities of a good mail seller. These qualities can be stated in reverse to determine what *isn't* likely to be a good mail seller. A product is not usually suited to mail selling if it carries a profit margin of less than forty percent, and even that may be too small a margin. A product is not suited to mail order unless you have a steady source of supply for it. It is not suited to mail order if it is complicated and requires elaborate explanation and instruction for its satisfactory use. Products that sell for over $10 are not ordinarily good mail order products (although there are outstanding exceptions to this rule, as there are to the others given). Items which are sold widely in retail stores are not good mail order products unless they are given some unusual sales twist. Nor are items which do not open the door to a future repeat sale to the same customer, either of the same product or a similar product.

Chapter 26

What You Should Know
About the Post Office

All mailing pieces that originate in the United
States for delivery to destinations within the United
States fall into one of four general classes: First Class,
Second Class, Third Class, or Fourth Class.

First Class mail is probably the class most familiar
to you if you have not had previous mail order experience. Into this class fall personal letters, postcards,
business-reply envelopes and cards, and other types of
mail which you may elect to send first class by paying
first-class postage.

Second Class mail is a class set up to accommodate
publishers of newspapers, magazines, and other peri-
odicals that qualify. This allows them to enjoy fast
distribution of their issues at a very nominal cost.
Complaints are continually being registered with the
government about publishers getting a "free ride,"
mailing at the expense of the taxpayer. It is undoubtedly true that taxpayers bear a good part of the postage
bill for publishers, but there is another important
factor to consider in the matter; that is, if they were
not allowed to mail cheaply, most publishers would
be forced out of business overnight. This is not a
desirable thing to happen, since the freedom of our

country depends in large part on freedom of the press and wide dissemination of news and knowledge. As a mail order operator second-class mail will rarely if ever come into use or consideration; but as a United States citizen, it is important to have an understanding and appreciation of this special class.

Third Class mail is the catch-all for business mail and everything that doesn't go by one of the other classes. The main purpose of the third-class provision is to give mass mailers an economical means by which large quantities of purely commercial mail can be distributed. As a mail order operator you will be more concerned with this class than any other except parcel post.

A letter that travels third class gets to its destination almost as quickly as a first-class letter (except during the big rush seasons, such as Christmas), but costs about one-half as much to mail. If you are on anyone's mailing list, particularly as a magazine subscriber, you no doubt are deluged with sales letters from many other magazines wanting you to subscribe to them, also. The majority of the letters you receive of this kind will have been mailed third class. This class also includes catalogs, circulars, pamphlets, broadsides, self-mailers, and other pieces which do not have the characteristics of personally written correspondence.

There are several identifying marks of a third-class letter. For one thing, it must be so identified somewhere on the outside of the piece, or it must bear a notation that the postmaster may open it for postal inspection. It will usually have printed indicia rather than a postage stamp, said indicia showing the third-class permit number, city, and state. Some mailers decorate these indicia or otherwise dress them up to the point where they appear at casual glance to be official postage stamps and cancellations.

Matter which is sent by third-class mail may be reproduced by any method or mechanical process, with the exception of personal handwriting. That is, anything that is printed by letterpress, photo-offeset, mimeograph, spirit duplicator, etc. may be mailed third class. This includes letters that are reproduced individually on automatic typewriters, provided all letters are identical in wording except for the filled-in name and address.

A limited amount of personalizing is permitted in third-class mail, and this includes individually signing letters or applying the signature with a rubber stamp.

There is a restriction to third-class mail which limits the weight of a single piece to sixteen ounces or less. Any letter or parcel which weighs in excess of that amount must be sent by parcel post.

Third-class mail also includes bulk-rate mailing privileges that are especially valuable to those firms who mail many thousands or millions of pieces per year. While you can get a permit to mail third class free of charge, you must pay an annual fee of $30 in order to enjoy the bulk-rate privileges. (To use the printed indicia, rather than precancelled stamps or postage metering, you must also pay an additional $10 fee.)

To qualify as bulk mail the letters must be mailed no fewer than two hundred at a time, and they must all be identical in appearance and wording, except for the addresses, of course. In addition, they must be sorted by state and city, with a minimum of ten pieces for each town or city, and must be tied in bundles prior to delivery to the post office. To the big mailer this sorting and tying (normally a post office function) is a small price to pay for the excellent savings made in postage.

Of course, in the beginning you may not be ready or willing to go in for heavy bulk mailing. You may have only a few dozen or a few hundred letters to mail third class. Without paying any special fees, you may mail them at the third-class rate by identifying them as third-class mail (with a rubber stamp or other means) or by leaving the flap unsealed. In such a case, you would affix precancelled stamps, available at your post office, and mail the letters in batches of twenty or more. It is not necessary to sort your letters by city and state when mailing in this manner.

Fourth Class is also an important class to the mail order businessman. This is another term for parcel post. If you know what parcel post is, you know what fourth-class mail is. Nearly anything can be mailed by parcel post if it is not specifically prohibited (such as whiskey, firearms, and contraceptives). This includes virtually every kind of merchandise, books, and catalogs weighing over sixteen ounces.

A parcel post package may not include any personal message, such as a letter to the customer, but it is permissible to include an invoice that has been individually written or typed. In general, if you are selling a legitimate product by mail, it is a safe bet that the same can be shipped by parcel post, subject only to the prevailing weight and size limitations. (Twenty pounds and seventy inches, respectively . . . but if there is any doubt about a particular package, ask your post office.)

If you have ever mailed or received anything by parcel post, you have probably noticed that the postage was governed not only by the weight of the parcel but also by the distance it had to travel. The farther it goes, the more it costs. (This isn't true of letters or postcards.) The Post Office Department has set up a standard scale of distances known as postal zones, and the United States is divided into eight of these zones. The zone in which you are located is your local zone, and packages mailed within your community get the local-zone rate. Zones 1 and 2 include everything within a 150-mile radius of your location, and the rest of the zones comprise ever-widening radii of distances from you. Zone 8, for instance, includes those places that are 1,800 miles or more from you; Zone 4, those that are 300 to 600 miles away.

This business of zones may be confusing to you until you have begun to mail packages out. After you have mailed a few orders, though, you'll have it pictured clearly in your mind. In case you want to determine the amount of postage your packages require, before you take them to the post office, there are zone-and-postage charts available. Most postal scales have a built-in zone scale which automatically tells you how much postage is required provided you know the distance from mailing point to destination. Most office-supply stores and many post offices have ready-made distance-and-zone charts that will simplify the task for you.

A *business-reply permit* is one of the most useful things in mail order, whether you are selling by direct mail, catalog, or inquiry follow-up. As you already know, to get the maximum number of orders from your mailing pieces, you must make it easy for your customer to order. One way you do this is by enclosing a business-reply envelope for your customer to return his order in.

A business-reply permit number is yours for the asking. You merely fill out a brief form, and when it is approved (a matter of a few minutes), you are assigned a number. You then take this number to your printer and have him print a supply of business-reply envelopes (or cards, if that is what you prefer). These envelopes and/or cards have to be printed to conform to a prescribed appearance and size, but most printers have standing forms to go by and need only your permit number, name, and address to do the job properly.

When a business-reply envelope comes back to you from a customer, it will come postage due and cost you two cents more than you would pay for a first-class postage stamp. However, since every envelope that comes back contains an order, you will find that you don't mind paying the small premium. And by using the business-reply form, you'll also find that you receive more orders than you would otherwise.

While most of your customers will send cash, check, or money order, a small percentage of them will ask you to send their order C.O.D. You don't need to be told that this stands for "collect on delivery" and that the postman on the other end of the line collects from your customer, then sends you a money order for the amount involved. There's nothing to shipping C.O.D. except that it takes a little more time than regular shipments. And it costs an extra handling fee, over and above the postage, which you may pass along to your customer.

A C.O.D. package must not differ from any other form of parcel post; the same regulations apply. The only difference is in the way in which you get your money. No C.O.D. package may be sent collect for more than $200, however.

The mechanics of shipping C.O.D. are simple. The post office will provide you with C.O.D. tags and show you how to fill them out. You merely attach a tag to each C.O.D. package and present it to the parcel post window. The post office will do the rest. You do, as you'll learn, have to pay the parcel post and C.O.D. fees in advance, when you mail the package. But you can be reimbursed for these by adding them to the amount the post office collects from your customer.

A post office box is a handy thing to have in the mail order business, if for no other reason than that it permits you to get your mail on Sundays and holidays. (There's no suspense like having to wait an extra day or two to get your mail when you're in the mail order business.) A box doesn't cost much, and anyone is entitled to one provided it is to be used for a legitimate purpose. In some cities, however, there are more people wanting boxes than there are boxes to go around, and in such an event you usually have to put your name on a waiting list.

Boxes are rented on a quarterly, semiannual, or annual basis. And the rental fee is payable in advance. (There's no credit at the post office.) The use of a box has its disadvantages, especially for a new, unknown mail order firm. Prospective buyers hesitate to send money to a firm using only a post office box number. After you become better established and acquire a reliable name, the use of a box will not affect your business to any appreciable degree.

Your post office offers many other services besides those described here—such things as money orders, insurance, special delivery, air mail, stamped envelopes and simplified addressing lists. Remember, the post office is there to help you and serve you. Don't hesitate about going to it when you have any kind of question or problem. When you're not sure whether a piece should be mailed third class, fourth class, or first class, take a sample of it to your postmaster and he will tell you how to mail it. This applies to any other postal matters that come up. If your local post office can't answer a specific question, they will get the answer for you from Washington. When in doubt, always ask the people at the post office. They'll help you out, and it won't cost a penny.

If you really want to delve deep into the workings of the Post Office Department, you can buy a copy of the *United States Official Postal Guide, Part I* from the Government Printing Office, Washington, D.C. Or you can see a copy free at your local post office.

For regulations pertaining to advertising claims, types of prohibited merchandise, etc., you should refer to a copy of the *United States Postal Laws and Regulations,* also available from the Government Printing Office or at your local post office.

On the subject of regulations, remember that Uncle Sam and his Post Office Department do not want to be a party to any fraud or deception. Therefore, they will not knowingly handle any mail or merchandise that is tinged with fraudulence, misrepresentation, or deceit. Don't take any chances; the postal inspectors are clever men. Besides that, it's foolish to get involved in a shady enterprise when it's just as easy—if not easier —to make money honestly.

Chapter 27

What You Should Know About Copyrights

As you may have observed, and as we have stated before, the easiest, safest, quickest way to build up a paying mail order business is to sell something which you create yourself or someone creates for you.

The reason is this: When you sell your own product, you have complete control over its distribution. No one can buy it except from you. You have no competitors in that exact product. The entire nation is your market.

You don't have to be a marketing expert to realize that it is better to have the whole cheese to yourself than to have to slice it up among a dozen or a dozen dozen competitors. When you handle your own offering, over which you have exclusive control, you do not have to divide the cheese with anybody.

There are several ways to get control of a product that has such priceless exclusiveness. One is to design and manufacture (or have manufactured to your specifications) some unique device, gadget, or other consumer product of a tangible nature. But this method involves long, drawn-out patent searches and applications, expensive tooling and manufacturing, and costly

promotion. All of which is O.K. if you have the time
and money to devote to it.

Another way to get a product that no one can sell
but you—and no one can buy except from you—is
through the written word. And when you sell the
written word, your exclusive control over your product
is assured by *copyright.*

It is no accident that there are probably more
firms selling books, courses, and manuals than any
other single class of mail order goods. The reason they
do is simply that only through copyrighted publications
can they achieve originality and exclusiveness of product cheaply. and with little risk.

Thus, if you want to take the shortest route to
getting an exclusive product, do it through writing . . .
and copyright what you have written. You don't have
to be a creative writer or even a journalist. If you have
an idea for a course of instruction, a self-help manual,
a money-making folio . . . jot down the things you
know in orderly, readable form, print the work, copyright it, and sell it.

This is rather a long prelude to the subject of copyrights, but the purpose of approaching the matter in
this oblique fashion is to impress upon you the value
of copyrights in the mail order business and to encourage you to take advantage of them. If you already
have something to sell—if you're not interested in selling the written word—then, of course, you probably
will not have read this far.

Copyright covers a multitude of creative and non-
creative sins. Such things as dramatic compositions,
songs, works of art, and photographs all come within

the domain of copyright. We are concerned here with only one classification, however, and that one is labelled "books."

In the language of the copyright office *book* means just about anything committed to paper and reproduced by mechanical process. A book can be a catalog, a booklet, a leaflet, a pamphlet, a brochure, and so on. But to the copyright office it is still a book. For all practical purposes, the term "book" covers just about everything you will encounter in the mail order business.

The procedure for getting yourself a copyright is as follows:

1) Write to the Register of Copyrights, Washington 25, D.C., and request the proper forms and instructions for copyrighting a book.

2) Get your particular "book" (manual, course, booklet, etc.) printed, and include the copyright notice in the front, on the title page or verso. The copyright notice reads as follows: Copyright 19........(year of publication) by................................(your name).

Bear in mind that you print your work with the copyright notice on it before you file for a copyright. You cannot copyright anything before it is published.

The final step in copyrighting is:

3) As soon as your "book" comes off the press, take two of the best copies and send them, along with the proper fee and the copyright application forms, to Copyright Office, Library of Congress, Washington 25, D.C.

That's all there is to getting a copyright. It has an initial duration of twenty-eight years. In the final year you can apply for a renewal, and have your copyright extended for another twenty-eight years. At the end of fifty-six years the copyright ceases to exist and the work belongs in the public domain, and can then be copied, published, and sold by anyone who chooses to do so.

A copyright is yours to do with as you see fit. You can publish and sell the work yourself or you can grant someone else the privilege of publishing and selling what you have written, in exchange for a flat fee or a royalty based on the selling price. Since a copyright represents a valuable piece of property, it can be willed to heirs, who can exploit it as they see fit within the fifty-six-year limit.

When you assign or sell the rights to a work in which you have copyright, the agreement must be in writing, and it must be recorded in the Copyright Office within three months.

The word "published" as used in the above context is a general term covering all conventional reproduction processes. It does not mean that your work has to be printed on a printing press and bound with a leatherette cover. Instead, it can be produced by any of the economical processes, such as mimeograph, spirit duplicator, and offset, and still be considered as having been published. No fancy covers are needed. In fact, you don't need any covers at all. The first page can serve as the cover, if necessary.

You can get a comprehensive outline of the copyright law by sending fifteen cents to the Register of Copyrights, Library of Congress, Washington, 25, D.C.

Chapter 28

Some Do's and Don'ts
for Mail Order Operators

Do set yourself a guiding rule of absolute honesty when you enter mail order work. It is the only safe way, the only satisfying way, to conduct a business by mail.

Don't pretend to be something that you are not. False fronts serve no useful purpose. Certainly they do not impress anyone but the most gullible.

Do give your company a name which fits the nature of your operation without implying nonexistent facilities or inordinate size.

Don't call yourself a manufacturer unless you really *are* a manufacturer. Don't call yourself a printer unless you *are* a printer. Don't call yourself an importer unless you *are* an importer. And so on.

Do use your own personal name in your firm name when an assumed name would sound ostentatious and unreal. "Jones Mail Order Co." sounds more plausible than "Amalgamated Mail Enterprises."

Do visit your county clerk when you start doing business, whether you use just your own name or an assumed name. In either case, it is wise to register the name with the county clerk, and in some states this registration is required by law.

Don't fail to investigate the laws of your state regarding the sale of particular items. While there is no federal license required to do business by mail, some states require certain licenses and put a tax on certain classes of goods. Your local tax-assessor can help you in these matters or at least refer you to the people who can.

Don't begin selling taxable items until you've determined how much tax is required and whether it is to be paid to the state or federal governments. In most instances you will be acting as a dealer, and your supplier can apprise you of the tax situation regarding a particular product. Generally, such taxes are passed along to the consumer, although you may have to keep account of them and make periodic remittances to the government.

Don't risk your reputation and mail order career by handling an item of questionable nature or value. There are too many good things around to sell without your having to handle any product that cannot be ethically sold.

Do guarantee your products and stick with the guarantee. A good guarantee can build a business rapidly; a guarantee that is not honored will drive customers away, create ill-will, and possibly result in charges of misrepresentation.

Don't say anything, or allow anything to be said, in your ads and sales literature that is not the truth. It isn't necessary to distort, exaggerate, or mislead to make sales. On the contrary, more sales will result when you deal in facts and present them sincerely. This does not preclude, of course, a certain amount of "romance," or putting the facts in the best possible light.

Do stand ready to go to any reasonable length to placate an unhappy customer. Return his money, replace his merchandise, apologize for the misunderstanding—but under no circumstances get hot under the collar and write him a stinging letter telling him what an unreasonable jerk he is for complaining about your products. Your biggest stock-in-trade is goodwill and the continued patronage of satisfied customers.

Don't use a letterhead that visually implies that you are anything but what you are. If you occupy a cramped office on the umpteenth floor of the Zilch Building, don't photograph the entire building and print the picture on your letterhead as though you occupied the whole place.

Don't get involved in any "trust schemes," whereby you send your products out to people who did not order them, with a request that they keep them and pay for them. While sending goods out on trust is not illegal, it nevertheless is frowned upon by the postal authorities. If a product is not good enough to be sold competitively, then you have no right to unload it on a trust basis.

Don't manipulate the prices of your products to make it appear that the customer is getting a price reduction when he actually is not. If you say that an item previously sold for $5.95 and is now going for $2.50, be absolutely sure that such is the case.

Don't state that a patent medicine or preparation is a "cure" for anything. In making claims for medicines and stock remedies, you are on very dangerous ground. You can't make any claims that cannot be substantiated by scientific proof . . . and *you* have to do the proving. In selling any product to be used in the treatment of the human anatomy, you must know exactly what you are doing. Nor does it relieve you of responsibility to be merely acting as agent for another manufacturer or distributor.

Do remember these rules when labelling a formula or preparation that you intend to market:

1) Information that appears on the label must also appear on the package or be legible through it.

2) All information on the label must be easily seen and not obscured by pictures or other matter.

3) All information required on the label must be printed in English, though a foreign language may be used in addition to English provided the same information appears in that foreign language.

4) The label itself must give the name and address of the manufacturer, distributor, or packager; must tell the quantity of the preparation in the package; must describe and state quantity of habit-forming drugs if such are contained; must give the common or usual name of the drug; must give names and proportions of each drug used in compounding; must give adequate directions for use; must provide warnings against unsafe use by children; must warn against excessive amounts and lengths of time; must indicate limits of therapeutic value.

(*Note:* For detailed information concerning labelling and advertising a proprietary drug or medicine, consult the Federal Trade Commission.)

Don't use testimonial letters in advertising when they do not give a true picture of the facts. Some customers are so anxious to see their names in print that they will say anything about a product, whether it's believable or not.

Don't handle sex books (unless they are of an unquestionably authoritative nature), glossy photos of undraped Hollywood starlets, party movies, naughty postcards, pornographic novelties like the famous Mexican "man in a barrel," or any other kind of erection set. Quite apart from any moral issue that might arise, it just isn't good business. In the first place, the field is overcrowded and the competition is keen. In the second place, there probably isn't as much profit in it as you may think.

Chapter 29

Your Business Organization

There are three general types of business organizations or ownership: *sole proprietorship, partnership,* and *corporation.*

If you are planning to finance your business yourself, run it yourself, and take all the profits yourself, then you will own the business yourself, and this type of ownership is known as "sole proprietorship." This is the commonest form of business organization, and most small mail order businesses fall into this category.

There are several advantages to being a sole proprietor. For one thing, you are not obliged to take advice from or share managerial duties with a partner. You make all the decisions yourself without having to consult anyone, unless you wish to. At year's end if there is any profit, it all belongs to you. Also, as a sole owner you are not faced with the complications which arise from the legal technicalities of a partnership or corporation. In most states the law does not require you to file any formal documents when you are doing business as a sole proprietor. You simply register your name with the county clerk and start doing business.

There are a couple of disadvantages, however, to running a business with only yourself as owner. One of these is that you are limited in the amount of capital you can raise to put into it. There is no partner to call upon when you need extra capital, and since you are not a corporation, you can't float a new issue of stock to raise more money.

In a sole proprietorship you as an individual are wholly responsible for all of the company, and this can affect not only your business credit but your personal credit as well. In a partnership the debts are assumed on a proportionate basis between or among the various partners.

While most mail order businesses of modest size require a fair amount of capital, they don't always necessitate taking in a partner. About the best reason for entering into a partnership is to have someone around who can share the work and assist in managing the business, as well as someone who can contribute additional skills and ideas. Ideal partnerships are often worked out between partners who have complementary skills; for instance, a person who knows production might profitably team up with someone who knows advertising and sales.

If you do form a partnership with one or more people to carry on a mail order business, you will be wise to get the terms of the partnership down in writing. This takes the form of a *Partnership Agreement*, and the only sure way to get such a form executed properly is to have it prepared by a lawyer. You can, in some cases, get by with a simple oral agreement between yourself and your partners. But unless you know them extremely well, it is best not to rely on oral agreements; because if the business founders and sinks, there should be no room for disputes as to who is going to pay what.

A corporation is a business form very much like a partnership, except that the partners are known as *shareholders,* and they are not liable for the failure or success of the corporation, or any of its obligations. In the eyes of the law a corporation is an entity in itself, and the human beings involved in the operation of it are merely the implements that are used to make it function.

To organize a corporation, you must first pass rigid muster with your state government. In most states the Secretary of State is the agent who handles corporation matters. Once having made application and passed muster, the state grants you a *charter* under which you are allowed to issue and sell stock for the purpose of raising the capital needed to start and operate the business.

Corporations are unwieldy for the most part, from the viewpoint of the average mail order operator, and it is a good idea to postpone any incorporation plans you may have until you get the business off the ground. After it has become successful, it is an easy matter to incorporate if it should appear advantageous to do so.

Chapter 30

The Perfect Mail Order Product

The *perfect* mail order product probably does not exist. But if you should ever run across one, in all likelihood it will possess the characteristics listed below. Any such list, of course, is subject to many successful exceptions, but nevertheless, it is a guide worth knowing and using when you are making a product search.

The Perfect Mail Order Product

—is not sold in retail stores at all, or to only a limited degree.

—is one which sells for three-to-four times what you have to pay for it.

—is one which is in demand by a fairly large segment of the over-all population.

—is one which is readily understood by the prospect, without necessitating lengthy instruction or education in its use.

—is one which sells in the $3 to $10 price range.

—is one which generates a demand for more of the same product or creates a desire for additional products of similar kind.

—is one which doesn't go out of style, doesn't deteriorate, doesn't spoil while in storage.

—is one over which you have exclusive production and/or distribution control.

—is one which has some distinctive, exclusive, or unique feature about it to set it apart from competitive items of a similar kind.

—is one which can be packed and shipped in readily available packing materials, with a minimum amount of damage in shipment.

—is one that can be mailed or shipped for a postage cost not more than ten per cent of its selling price.

—is one that can be backed with a strong guarantee without resulting in excessive returns.

Chapter 31

Getting in Touch with Suppliers

Getting yourself established with sources of supply (manufacturers, wholesalers, etc.) is a relatively simple matter provided you observe certain rules of good business practice. In many cases you will be dealing with relatively large firms, and it is apparent that such firms do not wish to get involved with amateurs, hobbyists, or others who appear to have no chance of becoming good, steady dealers.

Most manufacturers and distributors are anxious to do business with you, however, if your correspondence with them indicates that you know what you are doing and show promise of developing into a consistent buyer of their goods. As a matter of fact, you will be better off not attempting to buy wholesale at all until you have definitely made up your mind that you are going into business and intend to handle a certain class of goods. If you are already established as a retail dealer, of course, then these pointers will offer nothing new to you.

The first requirement, perhaps the only indispensable requirement, of a new mail order business is a businesslike letterhead. Such a letterhead should tell 1) who you are; 2) where you are; 3) the nature of your business; 4) your telephone number; 5) your correct mailing address. A few dollars spent on having a professional-looking letterhead prepared for you will decidedly pay off in the long run. To begin corresponding with prospective suppliers without such a letterhead marks you as an amateur or an individual who is trying to "get it wholesale" for his own personal use. In either case, you are not likely to get much response.

The second important rule in getting established with suppliers is this: Always *type* your letters neatly, accurately, and in a prescribed letter form. This may sound trite, but you'd be surprised how much weight an attractively typed letter carries with the people on the other end of the line, especially if you have never met them or had any personal contact with them in the past.

The third rule is, Get to the point quickly. Don't beat around the bush. State exactly what you want, whether it's a catalog, price list, or just information. These people are busy and are more likely to respond quickly to a letter that is brief, to the point, and specific.

The fourth rule is, Make it easy for them to reply. If they are known to charge ten cents or twenty-five cents for their catalog, then send the money along with your first letter. In writing for information about a specific product, or for information of any kind, enclose a stamped, addressed reply envelope.

The fifth rule is, Keep a carbon copy of all correspondence with suppliers. This will eliminate any possibility of future disputes or misunderstandings.

Two specimen letters are supplied here. One of

them is for use in requesting general information; the other, for use in locating a supplier of a particular item. You can use the letters as is or modify them to fit a special situation. At any rate, they are yours to use, and they have been proved to be effective in accomplishing their purpose.

Specimen Letter A

To be used when making original mail contact with a prospective supplier. Letter can be changed to fit any similar situation. Type on your own letterhead.

Date

Name of Supplier
Address
City, State, Zip Code

Gentlemen:

We wish to offer our retail mail order customers new products, of merit and value, that are in good supply.

It is our understanding that you have one or more items that are well suited to our program, and we are writing to request a catalog or descriptive literature on your line, as well as a schedule of dealer discounts and delivery information.

Since we sell through mail order channels, we naturally cannot take on new items indiscriminately, because our products must measure up to a set of mail order standards of price, appeal, weight, and so forth. However, the items we do select have a potential for enjoying a large volume of sales, and for this reason we can give you reasonable assurance that substantial purchases will be made from time to time.

Until such time as satisfactory credit arrangements can be made with you, all purchases will be made on a cash-with-order basis.

Thank you for an early reply.

Yours very truly,

Your Name

Specimen Letter B

To be used when you wish to find a supplier of a particular item. Type on your letterhead.

Date

Name of Firm
Address
City, State, Zip Code

Gentlemen:

We are trying to establish a source of supply for (name of item, description, etc.), and it is our understanding that you may be able to supply us with this product from your regular stock.

Purchases of this item, should we be able to locate a satisfactory source, will be made from time to time, for purposes of resale through mail order channels.

On receipt of information from you, and contingent upon suitable discounts and delivery schedules, we shall be glad to place an initial order.

Should you not be able to supply this item, we would greatly appreciate your referring us to another possible supplier.

Thank you for your prompt attention.

Yours very truly,

Your name

Chapter 32

Mail Order Record Keeping

Like any other business, mail order requires accurate, systematic record keeping. This includes day-to-day and month-to-month sales and expense records, as well as the added detail of listing keyed orders and inquiries, and recording direct-mail test results.

The basic purposes of a good record-keeping program are 1) to tell you whether you are making or losing money, and how much; and 2) to make it easy to file your income tax returns when the time comes. Also, there will be times when you will want to tally up your real worth, your "net" worth, for the purpose of establishing bank credit or an enhanced credit rating.

Mail order records don't have to be elaborate; the main thing is to keep *some* kind of record of every transaction made, in such a manner that at a later date you can run totals and get a quick picture of what has been taking place in the business.

For a small fee a public accountant can help you set up a simple system that you can maintain yourself, or if you can afford it, you can—at a small monthly rate—have him do the work for you.

An alternative is to buy a stock bookkeeping system (the Ideal systems are excellent) from your office-supply store, selecting the one that best serves your particular need. Such systems are made for many different kinds of businesses and are available for $2.50 to $4.50 each.

If you want to keep your system as simple and uncomplicated as possible, here is a suggestion. Buy a conventional three-ring loose-leaf binder and a quantity of blank white sheets to fit it.

You then divide your book into four sections (identifying each section with a file tab). Section 1 is "Record of Orders Received"; Section 2 is "Record of Sales"; Section 3 is "Record of Purchases"; and Section 4 is "Record of Expenses."

All you need do then is take a ruler and pen or pencil and rule the sheets in each section into vertical columns and horizontal lines spaced wide enough apart to accommodate the items of information that are to go into the respective spaces.

Section 1, "Record of Orders Received," should have eight columns on each page. These columns should be headed, from left to right, as follows: Date Order Received; Name of Customer; Address; Amount Enclosed; How Remitted; Date Order Filled; Amount of Postage; Remarks.

Section 2, "Record of Sales," is ruled off in the same way, but has only five columns and headings: Date; Quantity; Amount; Description of Item; Remarks.

Section 3, "Record of Purchases," has eight column headings: Date Ordered; Received; Supplier; Item; Quantity; Unit Cost; Total Cost; Remarks.

The last section, "Record of Expenses," also has eight columns: Date; Description; Postage; Advertising; Printing; Office Help; Professional Service; Other Expenses. Make the "Other Expenses" column a wide one, since it is a catch-all for many miscellaneous expenses such as insurance, rent, and utilities.

With such a homemade record system faithfully kept and kept current, plus your bank deposit slips and statements, you can at any given time produce an accurate profit-and-loss, or financial, statement—at least until the business has grown to a point at which you need a full-time bookkeeper.

In this connection, it goes without saying that you should open a bank account in your company name right at the start, and any time a purchase is made—or bill is paid—do it by company check. Good bank records are as important as your other records, and a cancelled check is indisputable proof that a certain expense has been incurred and covered.

Chapter 33

A Check List of Mail Order
Costs and Expenses

At the start of your mail order career it is easy to overlook or ignore a number of costs and expenses which must be included in your records if a true picture of your operation is to be gained.

For example, the cost of your product is more than the unit cost you pay the manufacturer or wholesaler for it. Here are the cost factors that go into the total amount you pay for a product:

1) The basic unit amount paid the manufacturer or wholesaler

2) Allowance for those units damaged in shipment, replacement of unsatisfactory units to customers, refusal of C.O.D. units by customers, in-house deterioration and breakage, etc.

3) Cost of additional assembly work in your plant if same is required

4) Shipping charges to your plant or office from the supplier

5) Postage or shipping charges to your customer

6) Cost of packing and wrapping materials and labor

7) Storage costs

Aside from product cost there are a variety of overhead expenses which you will incur, and which should

be recorded in your record books. Among your overhead items will be these:
1) Rent
2) Salaries to employees
3) Salary to yourself and partners
4) Utilities
     a. Electricity
     b. Gas or fuel
     c. Telephone
     d. Water
5) Automobile
     a. Local deliveries to post office
     b. Business travel, etc.
6) Office supplies
7) Taxes
8) Insurance
9) Licenses if required
10) Accounting or other professional services

Your third big category of expenses is advertising.
Over and above the cost of the amount of newspaper
or magazine space you use, there will be these added
costs:
1) Printing
2) Engravings
3) Photographs and/or artwork
4) Typesetting
5) Photostats
6) Copyrighting service
7) Ad agency service
8) Mailing lists
9) Addressing, folding, stuffing
10) Postage

Chapter 34

A Short, Short Course
in Mail Order Procedure

The following is a reliable guide to operating a mail order business, with each point given in the briefest possible terms. This will also serve as a refresher course in everything that has gone before, and is supplied in this form for quick reference and periodic study.

1) Choose an unpretentious, easy-to-remember firm name.

2) Try to convey an air of informality and friendliness in your literature and advertising.

3) Use a street address for your mailing address in preference to a post office box if possible.

4) Select a product that has consumer appeal and is well made.

5) Try to select a product that fills a definite need.

6) Select a product that is not widely sold in stores.

7) Select a product that has something unusual about it.

8) Sell a product over which you have exclusive manufacturing or distribution control if possible.

9) Sell a product that leads to a repeat sale or an auxiliary sale.

10) Steer clear of attempts at manufacturing in the beginning if it is avoidable. (Better to farm out the manufacturing in small quantities than to incur expensive die and tooling costs.)

11) Choose items that have a strong element of "newness" about them in preference to items that have been repeatedly sold by others.

12) As you can, add additional items until you have a line; it is hard to make much money from one product.

13) After one item has proved to be a good seller, look around for a second item to start advertising, then a third, and so forth.

14) If there are personal services that go hand-in-hand with your product, offer them also.

15) If the product lends itself to sampling, by all means offer a small sample of it to your prospects for

a modest price, with credit for the cost of the sample to be applied to a larger order.

16) Choose products that are light in weight (less than twenty pounds after packing), so that they may be mailed parcel post.

17) Avoid having to buy custom-designed cartons and other packaging materials; handle items that can be shipped in stock containers available from your supplier.

18) Figure postage costs into your selling price if possible.

19) Make all shipments prepaid, except for requested C.O.D.'s.

20) Use a neatly printed shipping label that is large enough to accommodate all necessary information.

21) Address shipping labels by typewriter, not by hand.

22) Use labels that have "Return Postage Guaranteed" on them.

23) Try to establish sources of supply close to home if possible.

24) Don't continue to deal with suppliers who prove to be slow or erratic in making deliveries.

25) Pay all suppliers promptly on receipt of invoices, in order to earn the cash discount.

26) Order goods in sufficient quantities to get the best discounts commensurate with your capital.

27) Price your products in such a way that your customers will say they got their money's worth.

28) When selling direct from space ads, offer products in the $3 to $10 price range, and show your prices in round numbers or as close to them as possible. (Customers do not like to send heavy coins through the mail.)

29) Always offer a money-back guarantee on everything you sell.

30) When setting your selling price, figure in all costs relating to the product, not just the cost of the product itself. This will include freight in, packing, postage out, C.O.D. loss, etc.

31) Handle only those products that offer a substantial profit margin: not less than forty per cent, preferably sixty per cent or more.

32) Don't attempt to build a large volume of business with $1 or $2 items. Offer items in the $3 to $10 range, and after you have acquired a customer backlog, start mailing offers of much bigger units of sale.

33) Don't expect to make a killing, or even a moderate profit, from one ad. Plan to advertise consistently.

34) When using space ads, use a size of ad commensurate with the unit of sale; i.e., a low-priced item usually requires much smaller amounts of space than a relatively high-priced item.

35) It is better to run two small ads than one big one, in most situations.

36) Tailor the copy, illustration, and headline of your ad to suit the audience of the magazine you are using.

37) Measure a magazine's effectiveness by what it pulls during a one-month period, and use that figure for determining your cost-per-sale. (Even though, as usually happens, there will be a certain amount of "trickle in" for several months to come.)

38) Determine the number of orders you need to break even, and then use only the magazines which pull above the break-even point.

39) Find your break-even point by dividing your profit margin per unit (determined by subtracting your total unit cost from your selling price) into the cost of the space used.

40) Don't rush to change an ad that is pulling well; experiment regularly, but experiment slowly.

41) Test one thing at a time: first a different headline, then a different illustration, then a different layout, and so on. If you test more than one thing at a time, you won't know which change produced the different result.

42) Test more than one magazine at a time if capital permits; test more than one ad at a time, but be sure each is keyed.

43) Offer permiums whenever and wherever you can.

44) Always strive to get a repeat order from a customer who has bought from you at least once. The big profit in mail order is in repeat business.

45) Run an ad that proves to be successful without change until its pull has dropped to the break-even point.

46) If product and ad look good but ad fails to pull, test again with different price, then again with different head. If it still doesn't pull, swtich to another product.

47) Don't waste space in a mail order ad; it's too valuable.

48) Small space ads should be written in brief, punchy style with emphasis on facts rather than persuasion.

49) Don't use words or phrases that a mass audience won't understand.

50) Talk about your prospect, not yourself or your company.

51) Strive for conviction and sincerity in ad copy.

52) Give the customer explicit directions for ordering.

53) If you have sufficient profit margin to sell to retail dealers, also, ask for dealer inquiries in your space ads; then follow them up with a special dealer mailing.

54) Remember, every letter and package that goes out from you can be the vehicle for circulars and announcements on other products; use them.

55) Get a testimonial program going as soon as you develop a few customers; use best testimonials in ads and letters.

56) Never fail to key an ad, coupon, or order blank.

57) If in doubt, get expert help in composing ads and letters.

58) Use illustrations or photographs that show the product in its best light; use them to convey the products usage, not as ornament.

59) Study the ads in the magazine you are considering, and see how you can design yours to stand out among them.

60) The best mail order magazines and newspapers to use are those that already carry a lot of mail order advertising.

61) In line with the above, the best publications are those that already contain advertisements similar to yours.

62) Newspapers are good for making fast spot tests, but for the long haul your best bet is magazines.

63) As soon as you get a space ad campaign going, have a follow-up customer mailing ready, offering your customers one or more related products. Follow up by direct mail.

64) Right from the beginning set up the names of your customers and inquirers on stencils or address plates; if you cannot afford this at first, set them up on multiple gummed labels.

65) Don't hesitate to rent your customer and inquirer lists to other mail order companies provided they are not directly competitive. This is a good source of extra income.

66) File the names of your customers and inquirers alphabetically, geographically, and by year. Make sure each address includes the Zip Code number.

67) Employ an advertising agency, if possible, but make sure it is one that has had heavy mail order experience.

68) Ask a prospective agency to show you samples of successful ads and mailings they have produced.

69) Don't expect an advertising agency to work for nothing; they are entitled to ask for flat fees until your ad account grows to the point at which it becomes worthwhile on a fifteen percent commission basis.

70) When an agency-produced ad or campaign goes sour, ask for their opinion and recommendations, then give them a second chance. They may have made fewer mistakes than you think.

71) Don't say, "No C.O.D.'s accepted" in your ads; C.O.D.'s can be good business. To reduce refusals, ask for an advance deposit of $1 or more.

72) Don't be afraid of personal checks; very few of them are returned unpaid. Most people are honest.

73) Don't offer to sell on credit unless you are handling relatively large orders ($15 or more) have sufficient capital to carry the accounts, and have a sufficient profit margin to absorb a five-to-ten percent credit loss.

74) Don't argue with a customer; if he's displeased for any reason, either replace the merchandise or return his money in full.

75) Don't sit on a complaint, thinking it will disappear. (It will just get hotter.) Answer by return mail.

76) If a customer sends you too much money, refund the overpayment immediately. You will make a friend.

77) Work your customer systematically; don't let him cool off. Have something going out regularly—at least once a month if possible.

78) Offer free gifts or premiums to customers who will refer their friends to you.

79) If an ad or offer is successful for a while and then seems to "wear out," drop it but keep it in the file. After a year or so it is probable that you can rerun it with the same degree of success it had initially.

80) Keep accurate records of incoming orders and inquiries as to key, date received, etc. This will be invaluable in projecting future ads and campaigns.

81) Maintain accurate business records and accounts so that at any given time you can determine whether you are gaining or losing.

82) Pay special attention to the seasonal aspects of your various offers, expanding your efforts during the peak seasons and cutting back during the off seasons.